ALSO BY GILBERT SORRENTINO

The Darkness Surrounds Us (1960)
Black and White (1964)
The Sky Changes (1966)
The Perfect Fiction (1968)
Steelwork (1970)
Imaginative Qualities of Actual Things (1971)
Corrosive Sublimate (1971)
Splendide-Hôtel (1973)
Flawless Play Restored: The Masque of Fungo (1974)
A Dozen Oranges (1976)
The Orangery (1978)
Mulligan Stew (1978)
Aberration of Starlight (1980)
Selected Poems 1958-1980 (1981)

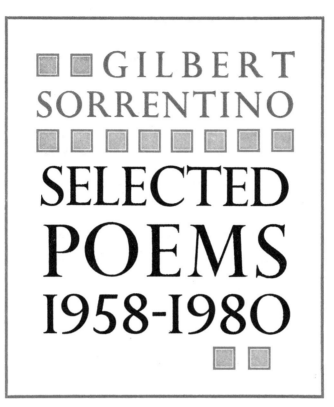

GILBERT SORRENTINO

SELECTED POEMS 1958-1980

BLACK SPARROW PRESS / SANTA BARBARA / 1981

ACKNOWLEDGEMENT

Grateful acknowledgement is made to the following publishers: Jonathan Williams Publisher (The Jargon Society) for poems from *The Darkness Surrounds Us;* Totum Press/Corinth Books for poems from *Black and White;* Black Sparrow Press for poems from *Corrosive Sublimate, A Dozen Oranges,* and *White Sail;* The Perishable Press for poems from *Sulpiciae Elegidia/Elegiacs of Sulpicia;* W. W. Norton & Co., Inc. for poems from *The Perfect Fiction;* and the University of Texas Press for poems from *The Orangery.* Acknowledgement is also made to the following periodicals in which some of these poems first appeared: *The Atlantic Review* (London), *Bad Henry Review, Invisible City, La Fusta, Mississippi Review, Parnassus, Partisan Review, Scranton Literary Review, South West Review* (England), and *Sun & Moon.*

LIBRARY OF CONGRESS CATALOGING IN PUBLICATION DATA

Sorrentino, Gilbert.
    Selected poems, 1958-1980.

    I. Title.
PS3569.07A17 1981   811'.54   81-1094
ISBN 0-87685-502-8   AACR2
ISBN 0-87685-503-6 (signed ed.)
ISBN 0-87685-501-X (pbk.)

Again, for Victoria

Contents

CORROSIVE SUBLIMATE (1971)

SULPICIAE ELEGIDIA / ELEGIACS OF SULPICIA (1977)

WHITE SAIL (1977)

THE ORANGERY (1978)

NEW POEMS (1978-1980)

THE DARKNESS SURROUNDS US (1960)

A Fixture

I've nothing to say
to them;

pride is as solid
as summer heat.

That is to say
you can't cut it:

with a knife in the kitchen
I cut

a tomato; nothing to say
to them: let them rot

and be bitten by night,
in the country.

I've nothing to say
to them. And I won't write.

Calling Dr. Dunninger

Falling asleep can be quite lovely
you put your head
on the couch.

The book falls
and the clock ticks
and the hell with the sandwich and milk.

Who's the character in the armchair
drinking cheap wine
glum as hell?

Nightpiece

Rats move swiftly along a wall,
they can frighten by moonlight;
while a mouse
can leap the rafters

of the house more
noisily, there is nothing
quite like a rat
blinded by nature

and fear, swallowed
by space, dead
center in the room;
you can see the moustaches

twitching. He doesn't know
which direction to take,
he is lost in the open area,
men have shot themselves

in the head
for less reason.

The Totem

They move beneath it
forward and backward
and they die for it,
often in smoke and sunshine.

Others tear their
guts out or their brains
on rocks and tin cans
in the swimming hole.

Whichever way it faces
or they face it, it has
its special misery, and it
costs plenty.

No help for it, though
each man knows
his lack: ask George Pickett, ask
Beau Jack.

3 Quatrains

When I say, love, it has
a meaning to it, not

a thing, that is an untruth, a
state, certainly,

"it was hot, fishing,"
proclaimed in December

is next to nothing to the
hearer, how can he comprehend

July? yet certainly it
was July, and was hot, as

much as love is when I say
it, hot, that is, but no thing.

The Crisis

That I cannot take
and that she will not

not give, but will not
have it taken. Something

like a brick wall is reached,
one can vault it, or

smash it down, there may be
another, taller, behind it,

or maybe not. Or maybe a
plain with sagebrush or fields

of sweetgrass and alfalfa, timothy,
was always a favorite word.

The Man in the Moon

Old man with whitening beard,
snapped once his fingers and the world
began, and with it, Mr. Moon, no matter
what the wise ones say,

the voyeur Mr. Moon, and the man
in him, with all those dirty postcards
taken of all us. To be bathed!
in milky light! to be kissed

in milky light! The flashbulbs
of that lecher in the moon, in
Mr. Moon, in Jules LaForgue's beloved
moon, beloved Mr. Moon:

and, wait'll you see this one,
says the man, wait'll you see
this, and what a joke it be, it's
someone that you love and that you did.

The Spouse

He came to the day that made him a hopeless husband
and he said to himself that he was indeed that husband
but what kind of husband

did the bitch suspect
he was? Could it be possible she suspected
that one day he would wonder, then suspect

her infidelities? He was incapable
of that suspicion, he was not capable
of his suspicions toward himself, his capabilities

concerned the pinning of beetles and birds
to a piece of black felt, watching seabirds and landbirds
and all sorts of animals also, he was a goddam fool.

Man and Wife

When it comes to the calling of names,
they were looking into the forest, birches
stood out among oaks and a couple of pines,

there are some I can think of for you.
A bluejay was chorus to this, and to
his silence,

the forest held close to
the morning, what names, his voice almost
drowned by the jay: what names?

What *names?* she repeated, and the
morning broke loose upon them, you
are a name too, he said, not what

I called you before: ha! she said,
and again, his voice then, you
are that forest right there, and your body

that bluejay, you are too much to know, you
bitch of a forest and jay, you
bleakhearted bitch of a morning, you

stillest birchtree.

A Señorita's Bouquet

I thought of the flowers I picked for her
coming home from the movies one night,
a metaphor in the eyes of the cat
in our alley.

Later I came across her dried corsage
from the wedding.
My heart so full of love
I crumbled the flowers,
a yellow dust like Bull Durham
clung to my fingers,
more softness to it
than her wedding flowers.

The Closet

Women are lost in the void
with the old souvenirs. We have
placed them behind

Xmas tree decorations, dusty
suits and old shoes, an older
love peers

from red string, there is
that girl, in a brooch, a
prayerbook holds up

my mother, who smiles at me
and is seconded, smiling,
my wife in a photo.

Midnight Special

We went through the hedge
and into a garden, my roses
were there, then things became
slanting snow.

In the center my son, cold
and crying. I was angry
with him, his tears
a reproach. Waking,

the sound of the clock,
and his breathing.

Over his bed I wept,
that he should be so helpless
and I as helplessly vindictive: child,
shine your everloving light on me.

A Classic Case

The moon's a little arch
pasted on black cardboard
just outside his bedroom
window,
          lovely Major Hoople.

I swear the room is warm,
the night is cold, the bedspread
turned down has a comfortable
feel,
          lovely Major Hoople.

Tomorrow he'll get up, put on
his fez, and stand behind
his gut, the sagging furniture
his friends,
          lovely Major Hoople.

Yow! That world
of yours is crumbling away,
the rotary lawn sprayers and The
Neighbors,
          lovely Major Hoople,

when will they possess
your useless yard and send
you out to work, to
work!
          lovely Major Hoople.

The Zoo

Goliathus goliathus, the one banana
peeling beetle in the U S A, brighter
than a comicstrip, is dead.

"Wrapped in his native grasses," left
on the doorstep of the museum
and a favorite of the visitors,

4 and 1 half inches long with an
8 inch wingspread, bigger than
Skeezix, with a life more full,

peeling his bananas for survival,
unlike Mamie Mullins, unlike Moon,
who would be Skeezix but for

the environment, ah! Who cares
or believes in them at all, at all,
goliathus was better and he

not a native.

The Fights

The coal was blacker than coal
when it all came down on them,

into the shaft, into the tunnel
they worked. A slab of earth

moved into it and when they turned
it was there, 13,000 feet

of night. But they sang
against it, talked against it

and they beat it. Ate chunks
of it and beat it. Indians

made cakes of locusts and sat out
the plague: these recipes

are found in losers'
cookbooks.

The Whole World Coal

In the whole world coal
there are the remnants of old
lovers and old enemies,
made into anthracite, bituminous,

and pea. How strange to see
the sinews of a hand
now just a lump, or
a grand slab under

Pennsylvania. Even
the city is incorporated
in the plan. I too,
why be so superior,

I speak from
50,000 feet.

Tilt

We will have nothing
that lacks the formal evocation.

Ya! To crown you
with it. Nor should you
be afraid, what to fear

from the curtsy or the
handshake. Stroking his
long moustaches, he moved
quietly from them, steel

beams hung from the sky,
whatever will become
of the lyric,
that will become
of the I.

BLACK AND WHITE (1964)

Ars Longa

Le blanc souci de notre toile
—Mallarmé

Carefully as a man tying up tomato plants,
they will to be arranged, the words,
they are all our concern, as that bright
little chainsmoker knew,

what is said is better than said if the
page be impinged upon with power.
Pebbles in a stream, the rings
they cause are unimportant,

the memory of those rings, though,
aha, the remembrance of them the next time
that we hurl the pebbles, there is a
dumb comparison, they argue in the water

as against the water in the brain, the
stream of yesterday's disturbance. Etched
finely, they neither moan nor weep, the
words, they are neither the experience

nor the telling of it; a barrier of cellophane,
to enmesh you tenderly, or fiercely,
one is here! one there! one is in two
or three places at ——! or is it

yesterday, what is this, a poem?
a group of words, a monster of the
evening, it slouches mightily, it is in
full possession of the land and sea,

it fills our sail, it fills our sail,
it fills our sail, it fills
our sail, it fills our
sail, it fills our sail.

The Transcript

I am no tree
no dogwood, nor
red sumac, not
even crabgrass

am a man, a
support but not a
tree, feelings
in me flow in

blood and cartilage.
Do not use me
as flower, bush or
sapling, tree.

The Fiction

This fire moves. Upward, upward,
smoke moved by it, forward to the
sky. I am lost here, where

did we all come from, I listen
to this dear friend's history.
Words batter at me, the wine is

good. Words beg that I
nod my head, monsters
of the past are here

in the room, a sudden turn and
I will have trapped them. "What
a time that was." Here,

here, on my neck: to turn? God
help me should they have that
face, this face, what face.

Cards

It is black night, spades
and clubs are trumps, hard
to see, the cards on which
their colors agree are

also black. Some streak
of gulls against this is
what I need, some line drawn
in yellow. Even blue

would do. My eyes strain
at peering at this node
of darkness, I wonder why
I could not see it forming,

or question why I did not
question those who could,
as if they knew: they are
obscured as well as the world

in which they move, and
walk. I hear a voice which
God knows might be mine calling
for a diamond or a heart.

Dominoes

It's too obscure, it's as it were
a slab of pie a glass of icy milk
in summertime, that's what he thinks
she's brought to him

though I think differently.
What I think is a link in a chain
of rain that goes from April
to September, how wet the ground

gets! What you think is in
the shapes that chortle in your latest
paintings, you can't hide them
they are referential of you

but there he is too. There is pain
that is black and that brown stands for
pain, the bitter red strains to encompass
pain, my word

it has become our definition or
our shadowing, the sun won't even come
in country windows anymore, the city long
has swept itself toward black

the total is as if one might
walk in that say, August rain, to a barn
and see a father there
swinging in thin air.

Sinking, Swimming

She has put her hand
to the door, it swings
open, the sea visible

between her waist and
the crook of the elbow,
shouldering; when he came

nobody's business but his own.
Silence clamped on the room,
he imagines, the sound of wind,

of breakers, the pebbles skitter
among the shells. A
cramped quiet,

water grey between
her waist and arm,
she moves in to the

room. The door
moves to behind. The sea
is a snapshot.

Ave atque Vale

We are going away now,
goodbye, goodbye, we are
slowly leaving you, we
are disappearing in eddies

of smoke, the trees are
around us, and I know
you thought we would stay
but we are moving away

now, more swiftly, it
seems. We. Who moved
nowhere for so long, that
is a strange animation

there? It is I and
you, dear, we are leaving
ourselves now, slowly, see
our friends speaking to us

as we depart an inch
or two above the grass, I
can just see you there and I
beside you, goodbye.

The Meeting

1.

We all know too much of loneliness. I used to think
a man came stronger out of it. That might
be so. Testing the old vapidities
is not the same as saying them. They come at you
screaming, they cut up the soul,
injure you remorselessly: these things
that once lay under our surfaces waiting to be used
as objects to cause laughter, are become
fiends, they have northern eyes, blue
eyes, there is nothing at the bottom of them, they
sit in faces that leer obscenely, that take on
the faces, the shapes and declensions of friends. They
      speak
if you will listen to them, if you can
bear it.

2.

Caelum non animum mutant qui trans mare currunt,
not necessarily so, not at all so, or say that
the sky changes you. I picked up
pieces of petrified wood in Arizona, climbed
a mesa that had stood there 6 million years, it was
made of clay and rose coral, on top of it, I saw
as far as I could see in all directions, nothing: but
sky, but earth, but sky and earth, meeting, the
evil winds laughed at and past me. On the road you sat
in the car, the children in the car, your leg protruded
from the open door, and I was suddenly made barren,
    suddenly
a terrible aloneness, and the winds
frightened me.
           I thought I should not see you again,
the sky was full of blood and darkness, the blue was
the blue of the west, our west, deadly and implacable, it
    was
the eye of Satan, of all false gods, the evil eye.

3.

He said he could give up everything
except he could not give up anything
when the test was made of him. He
is a quiet man, I used to mistake

that for strength
when I was younger.
I mistook it for solidity
and thought all stronger

men were silent. I have always
talked, too much, and hated
it in myself. But what is speech
but the release of strength

that threatens to destroy us?
What is speech but
the incantation that can make
men out of mud and mountains

out of slime and nothingness?
"Still waters run deep," is a lie,
bring me the talkers, the windbags,
confessors and liars, the

men who talk all night and all day
who do nothing but talk, who
won't stop even when they have no more
to say, silence

is no more than the lid
of the garbagecan.

4.

I touched you, it was as if
I had never touched anything, you

were water, there was a smell of water
in your hair, your hands
were quick and nervous

fragile to hold and there was water
on them

I want to shatter the winds
that prey on us I reach

through years for your hand.

The Evening News

When you came, it was as if I saw you
through a window, there were people
around you, I caught edges of their shoulders
and arms within the frame.

                                    You stood directly
in the center and smiled at me like nothing
ever happened.

My smile was that smeary one
of the deaf and dumb, I offered
a dumb prayer
that bourbon was there,

it is not an out
but it puts you somewhere.

          Through a long winter of snow
and bitter sweepings of the wind I somehow
came through, not with you
but with her, upon whom I at length beamed
that same smeary face.

If there are such things as anger or disgrace
I have not found them here, in anyone I care
for, or in those I love. The calibrations
of these states are smudged so that I cannot tell
if they are fakes or actual precisions.

Anyway it all came out one color and one suit
as perfect as a flush, in spades. The night
drained through the hole the moon had made
and everything was clothed in grey.

The Charm

In a dream one sees it.
The touch is there, the taste
is there. The lips press
together, kiss air.

How can this man tell you
what skies hang over him?
How tell you
that you are in the sky

a gentle thing, a tender
thing? How say how much
his fingers hurt for you?
"It is only a dream of the grass

blowing." And that is
so. Only a dream created
by the grass, love bends it
and bends with it, love.

Bar Games

There was this glittering fuzz
of the quarter as it spun on the bar,
then doubled itself, I spun another,

the glitter cracked into a shimmering fall,
the quarter hit the wall of my glass
the other wore itself out. I don't care

how much it costs, I am waiting
for you, you are so beautiful it makes him
stagger and he is a queer. I don't wear

clothes for you but if they are there
so be it. Let's glut with alcohol
merriment has legs, caterpillars crawl

up, they crawl down trees, my God
the earth, these dazzling quarters
gauge the odor of you.

As with a Simple Gesture of the Fingers

three lives hung on two. A motioning
of fingers

and two rushed together. The rest
a construct, how high! how impossible
to see the top of it, it took so long
to make! And with the pointing of a finger
and two fingers, a swift line drawn in
air that lingers only in the lover's eye,

and all the bricks and spirings be dust,
be rubble.
                    I move my fingers, their
mechanics are familiar, where have I seen
such motioning before? and your fingers
are familiar to me too. Don't be proud,
I fight that imposition of my heart, this

is such a small outbuilding now, such
embarrassment to live in it, the dust
and relics heaped about, not yet moved away.

As with a simple gesturing of fingers
all my words are turned to singer's words,
held and polished for your unique delight.

The Long Goodbye

All night I spent turning
my head over my shoulder, turning
back toward those things that when they
happened I turned from, in a dodging

of pain, how well I avoided what
should have cut me, spilled, at least,
blood. I remembered my
voice, the texture of it

a weaving of shadows, the light
before thunderstorm. I am happy,
I said (the voice flashed its light),
happy. Sun in the garden.

The garden's movement in wind was
a palimpsest upon which your movement
also recorded—and I saw only the green of
the leaves, the ripening beans, the

tomatoes. You moved away in the sunlight.
Turning back over my shoulder, turning on
my back, my side, I cried into the dark
and she answered. Now God will me

and help me to feel all the pain
I must feel to become all the man that
I wish to become, and to make my voice
into a record of love with no turning.

The Bare Tree

It appears that each bare branch of this
sorry tree holds swaying a face

of me, the wind commands them in their
movement, the childish face that life

once gave to me is clear and perfect,
the exact old photographs my mother

took of me, what a stranger there
bending in the wind, changing

to someone just a little more like
I am now.

I give you those old visages, the clothes
too, time has thrown into its bag

and love along with them and along with that
whatever face I hold up to you now

and vow this face is honest, fragmented
only by the changes love forced into it.

Open Your Mouth and Say

Ah, how was I to know that the chink through
which I had to go to lay a finger or a tongue
on my own brain was so obscure so hidden so
infinitesimally picayune, I had thought
to do it by the numbers

other methods seemed to me immoral,
ludicrous or fine embarrassment.

The act though proved simply
pain, ah love, I had thought too
that the rain was tied up with the jinx.

It must be kept away! I hit a door,
my heart doublecrossed me into thinking that
these acts of love were capable of being
shut out, capable of seeming possible

as crossword puzzles. When will I learn
that abstract love for others puts a six

gun in the hand. When you cried the chink
gaped and became a wound, I think.

The Memory

A smell of apricots that brings a place
to mind. To the eye. Words twist in the air
in tortured anagrams

shards fall into your life
that once had meaning

you think. You are arrested and your face
is brought to bear on all of it. This man

that man. A woman is in it somewhere
for the asking but the apricots overpower
you, the sentences clamor, voices,
voices.

The air shifts, you thought you were
in the street, you are in a room, what room
can it be, it seems familiar, it is full
of a distant smell, sweet and thin
and these anagrams

are falling into patterns, of course you
are in a room, this is a smell of apricots.

They bring a place
to mind. These voices are meaningless,
are tortured problems twisting in air.

The Edges

My life is too full of faces,
my imagination too full of gestures
full as a garden is of leaves

and colors. Various movements
in my mind have counterpoint in reality

but I don't want that to be, the gestures
are too much for me.

Sometimes you feel your whole life leaking
out of you as if all your dearest things
were water, don't you find that so?

No one can help you then,
whether you are on the edges or roaring
in the center, your friends seem to be

armed against you and the faces of the drunks
are changed to knives. The question is

which knives are real?

Out of Their Butchered Hearts

They speak to you, give their love
for fearful interest. Look at
the pinfeathers on the windowledge

before accepting it. Or shuffle
the floor, mumble: red? green?
any colorings, turn to

white, request a black.
And one can quietly be seated, speak
of it in a civilized

vein, rather than a sudden
no, or an embracing. Out of their
mad, and butchered hearts

it is held out to you, moon
soft, jagged sun. The white walls
shake their finger smudges at you

take care that you do not
misinterpret them. They are mundane
symbols, and do not prove that

there is anything within you
that should take stock of these
various hearts: merely that people

were here.

The Mathematics

He stands before me. He must be
a friend for his hand
is proffered and his voice, but his head
is a blur
            like they draw speed.

He's hurt me so he must be a friend, that's
the simplest proof in the geometry I practice
which works on the assumption that when one
is stumped one can insert *Identity.*

See, he cries. That's because he's hurt
me and like a Christian true

and blue, it hurts him to see me hurt
and fumbling with my Q.E.D. improperly.

Maybe in the blur I understand to hold
his head there is a calculus

to demonstrate that the geometry itself
is obsolete and old.

So there are the clouds, do not believe them,
pure white or white with blue shadowing
or grey, black, remote, mixed with the smoke
from the stacks of the factory, I ask you
not to believe them, they portend a suavity
which will destroy, girdle a section of city
with a seeming peace and it is really puking
anger. Do not look at their shapes do not listen to
their shapes, don't think you can "hold them in your
hand." Nor think they "look like animals." Nor
initials, nor anything to do with blood, love,
a human warmth.

                They are dead
things
        and shape themselves toward death, they are
mist, cold,
freeze the brain
and the soul
emotions die in believing
of them.
                Don't go near
them, pull down the windowshade, their hypnotic
    shifting
will scramble your life, your brains will wither
and crackle, your loves will blow in
dust, borne on cruelty and laughter. They speak with
the voices of lovers and are lust, they have an odor
of marriage and are lust they are swirling with life
and death hides inside them, do not touch them do not
look at them, they are clouds, sunlight bounces from
    them
there they are/the clouds/do not believe them.

Faces of Doom and Sterility

confront him, the dead
faces rising out of the harbor, the mists
that lie on it, move across it with a sigh

moving over the waters. Confront him. Anger
him in their acceptance of that thing, that
doom, that sterile universe they inhabit, they sigh

these faces sigh, with soft voices, they are without
anger, wrath, pride or fury, they do nothing,
not well or badly, they do nothing. They

are blue, what crisp magic they work is to be feared,
it is blue magic, they mutate constantly, one fixes
them with a stare and they are gone, evanescent, moving

quietly over the waters, into the docks and warehouses,
gone across oceans in packing cases, the enemy. The
          faces
of misery sing to them but they are in themselves

misery, they seem to nod. All together, nod,
in agreement and commiseration. *Misericordia*
but it is not. It is sterility, guilt lies atop

each of us, an incubus, a succubus, we are afflicted
with Satan, who comes without horns nor in the
shape of the serpent but grinning and full

of understanding for each of us. As if he would say
what is your problem. Or did you say
(who spoke?) a Tuesday? I am here to help you

lying upon you in various guise, mostly a friendly monster, those faces out there on the waters (that move on the waters) are my hope and yours.

The Abstraction

The shape of the gesture,
the form of it before
it entered the blood
was silent, silently
it moved through the air

quiet enough for him
to figure its movement,
describe it to himself
while the blood
waited. His predictions

externally true, he was
tricked upon entry, it
turned to a color! He
could not see it, his
blood swirled around

and about it, but the
touch told him nothing
but black. Was it black
in the air, was it black
in the gesture it danced

in the air when he looked
at it silently moving in
air as it moved toward
the blood in a form made
of silence, and turned

to a color! A color
of blood which is black
as it moves as it feeds
the black brain and black
heart we all give a color.

The Language Barrier

There is a movement. Is it
a word that moves against
the air, the ear. It

is my own word I recognize
although the tones it encloses
are less strident than they were

in certain times of stress. It
moves with the flaw of the dance:
exists for myself alone, the

flaw of dancing measures and
explains it. I do not even know
this word, yet it moves in the

air toward my ear. Those who
might understand it are blind
to the motion. It should turn

with the fury of rats in a
trap, gnaw itself free of the
prison of space I have placed

it in. This prison it dances
in, dumb to the world, has
made it a thing with no

sound of its own, not real
to itself, not true to even
its stupid directions.

Who Goes There?

The vicious tight curl
of the pubic hair in the
bathtub, or a mass of black:

birds measuring the limbs
of a tree, these box in
a world full of demons

who are arrayed in black
in back of the world made
manifest in lusterless

porcelain, brass pipes
turned black and greasy
green, God damn those

nervous birds, the demons
possess them! They sway
—how long is that limb,

what grinning face inhabits
the friable leaf that
determines its tip—?

Someone, prove to me what
tender strategy will over-
whelm it, scrub it all

bright with the silvery
cables of bridges, tides
of love without logic

cracking the brittle
shapes the demons inform, forms
burned clean in a gout of flame.

A Detail

Where earth is, is also
water
        is not true of necessity.

Although where earth is, water
may be, poured on by a hand
holding a can
                or glass, or maybe
rain?
        From this we may infer, if
we be mad, or look into ourselves
crookedly: where love is, is also

those things which cause love—though
this is neither more or less true

than the paradigm above (of necessity). What

we come to know is that the wind blows
and the sun burns, legs take you places
if placed one before the other regularly.

There are other things, too, we know them
just as surely, but about

love, and water, earth and all simple things,
is is enough to find them out

simply, singly, make no mistake
about rules, it is possible to forget

even your children's voices.

Shapes of Winter

1.

To believe in a world of beauty: O
says the moon. The screech of the
birds answering the belief, the interjection
of the moon. A world of beauty,

silv'ry moon behind all of it, the light
turns to measure the crying
of birds, their crying inches toward
light, when they mesh, what

will occur? What world of beauty
occur, those black daubings spattered
on the moon revolve around

a stately ugliness, churn, settle.
Flight. My eye reflects a simple

bird-like movement, dumb hanging
world, lost in its bitterness of white, a
sad man's face hacked out of it.

2.

A smashed kite in a tree
its stars are bleeding
down on the grey coats and faces
moving beneath, let them
turn up their faces
and welcome it, the blood, do they

know that it's death? Let them turn up
their faces themselves, I can't, where are those
that rave
                    in a professional tone?

This collage on the door,
made out of busted newspaper, and its
stripes are bleeding down
on me. I don't know that it's death

it is simply, there.
                                What tokens
of love our crude hands
fashion, and break. Broken love,
bleeding in stars, bleeding in
stripes, blacks/whites, and

the red/white/blue of our
bunting.
                    Grey faces, muddled races
look at the dripping of death and

see in it love, so humbly fashioned
and so broken by our
fumbling hands.

3.

Shall I have it
pretty? Add a lake to it,

say that it shimmers, that
it glimmers. The sunlight
skids across it on the
wind. I'll have it pretty

or know the reason
wry. Birds hop among their
own droppings (strike that, I'll
make it pretty): among the

shafts of buttered sun
that la de da.

Here, "and here," is a piece
of orange glass, orange, yellow,
spectrum mellow, O the winter
settles in, I'll have it

by the hair, the razored edges
of the orange glass shall cut it
for me,
                in this shallow season
                I shall know the reason

why: to render it all up and
make it pretty, ah, this tarnished Shiva

glares at me—

4.

Grey settles
down, pearl lights
sway against the branches

that the wind
should sway

and out there is
love, soaked by
wind covered
in loneliness

but she knows

that love is not
grey and hangs to
the pearl gleam

of the lights that light
the park, the trees
they turn to marble

mocking spring and
all that saccharine
of green, that blast

of color, green for
envy, or the monster
whose head is truly

frightening, but each one
knows, a sight to look upon
or else our hearts may

stiffen to the marble
trees that should sway
in these auguries

of snow, that stand in
this scarred season, O
that stand so

5.

The edges of these buildings cut
the edges of the air and I
take what gloom upon myself?—

one year now since softer
weather, we all remember that
gentle temperature, Christmas
bells ringing through persistent

warmth. A miracle! A birth,
a virgin birth, ah, old friends,
their faces split in two with
merriment above their egg

nogs! A miracle! The edges of those
buildings blurred in sloppy
air, a miracle! How hot is it
in the Congo, you say a cold

front's moving in? What gloom
I take upon myself, 12 months of
brand-new life for me, the virgin
birth, a miracle! The edges of

these buildings frame the snow.

6.

The night of the first snow
a polar bear lumbered between us!

the snow was white against his
whiteness! and your eyes
were dark, ah! winter

wonderland, this stringent
city!

7.

(Dirty Glasses)

The delicate lacework of the fire escape
ends abruptly at the top and bottom of each rail
in whorls that remind me of eyes behind
spectacles that look out upon a wet and frozen
world. In whorls that hold in their centers
a delicate lacework of trees that remind me
of nothing but trees that are cold and depleted.
One black and rusted lace laid carefully upon
a brown and sodden lace is the true shape
of winter that I know. If I were to stand
in the park—what an amazing idea!—the lace
of the trees would lie upon the black and the rust
of the fire escape, the whorls would be whorls
and wouldn't remind me of eyes. Who sat in
the room that I wouldn't be in would contemplate
a wet and frozen world (seen through the window)

Silences

Out of a quiet mood of night
come women's voices, so far
away that they are the white
figures at the other side
of that dark lake in the picture
that hung in my hall as a
child. Now that I think
of it I know that they
were not people but sails
perhaps? Or rays of light
the painter squeezed through
leaves of the giant trees,
but in my mind they must remain
people, lost in the swift
evening that bludgeoned them
and drove them to the little
light remaining in the shimmer
remaining on water, and what
were they speaking of, and
what were their names, and now
though I hear their voices in
the night all I can tell for
sure is that they are women's
voices, soft and white, wrapped
in white vowels floating above
the white gowns that cover
their limbs, lost in the rushing
darkness of the summer evening.

THE PERFECT FICTION (1968)

Something plus something is not one thing.
An insufferable, vicious truth.
One lives with it or one dies. Happy.

He walks on the street, in
his life. The thunder
gives voice to the heat, a smell

of rain, and trees move.
The alley, cracks, a drain,
peach trees with hard, sour

fruit. The heat itself
a kind of dreadful thunder, trees
crack the sky up into

varied areas
of grey. He is drained, does not
wish to use his voice, one

line of peach sky
holds, in the west. There is
little for him to hold to,

his life, cracked, another
thunderstorm to mark
it: he walks towards home,

a remembrance of clatter,
pots and pans:
and now the rain. He is half

way down the alley, trees
lashed now: "It was late
in the evening when K. arrived." In snow.

In a fantastic light:
blue of hydrangeas, white
and pink. That light

before the evening starts
to come fast. The sweet smell
of rye and grasses, the

sounds of animals from
the barns, red, of course,
the hand up against

light touching the blossom.
Blue. It must be blue, the
other hand falling

away in casual gesture.
Innocent. The fantastic light.
Caught. Stiff. Concrete.

The stupid painter paints. He
sells his world, or what he thinks
is someone's world. Writers write

their junk, everybody drinks his
booze, is gay, adultery is just another
day in, day out minuet.

Behind this world, is nothing.
This world reveals itself completely—
the painter is a liar, the writer

wants to sell his books and fuck
somebody who says she loves
his work. What strength can I,

who feel these temptations pressing
on my very eyes, draw from these
images of lust, and of success?

It is a total darkness. It is
filled with women who are never
wrong, and when they make some

small mistake, stand in heels
and beautify the whole of day
and evening. God has allowed me

to see only me, and that sight
is enough to drive me to the sources
of a power, any power.

I have love in my hands, all
smeared, red, as in blood or lipstick,
years have deepened the color.

It is the same red that our friend,
the painter, paints. He smiles,
he whistles as he wastes my time.

What is past is here, as we
will summon it, so dead, but
    caught in the mind, sticky

and useless, an old song, half
of the words made up
    or hummed. The noble faces

of dead bourgeois who looked
their one time at a hired camera
    —some elegance has

shone forth from those
apathetic faces, the camera
    is there! to take a picture!

No candid or casual icons
but precise, they exist substantial
    in that flesh, those hired clothes.

They have some message
for us, straining we see
    dead fashions, white-gloved

hands thrust into pockets,
stylishly—the past thick
    concrete between us, heavy

and dark and intransigent,
the X'd window on some
    wrecked honeymoon hotel.

Now the night is here. Blood
will stain us, will sustain
us. Nobody's windows have

nothing nowhere behind them
anymore. A stupid face
is part of the pane—don't tell *me!*

Simple, and simply cold, dogs
are barking at the wind. The
lamp shows dirt ground into

the grain of the wood. Wherever
they have corpses, they have maggots:
maggots are only worms, most

of them love rotting lobster
and will feed on men. What wind
is blowing, an old woman who maybe

was kind to her cats is dying
of loneliness. Hers is that face
in the window, how impossibly

remote, how sad to consider it
as part of a pane of window
glass. The part of me I

think of as strength is
black, it is hollow: one goes on,
as one goes on, there is no

explanation. Any stupid bastard
laughs, some can even speak.
That can be a part of happiness.

I own the words I write, the
things I love are mortgaged, my
payments are all partial and erratic.

What intense colloquy with the self
will furnish—may be nothing. A
yawn is the reward. This clock,

dull in the room. Confrontation
with a beloved human being is
a superior achievement, is human, is

impossibly difficult. We buy anger
in this time, once in a great while,
a thought is thought. Clear and round,

oranges ripen on a little tree,
across the room, pure in their
orange, the implication of flavor

is intense. The smell of the
blossoms, on occasion, stirs some
fictive and banal nostalgia.

I sit, in my inviolate and
manufactured arrogance, my pen
moves familiarly, the clock,

the night, this light on light
blue lines, the white,
white paper filling with these

words—all at one with
the identical nostalgia, we
are all products of—

"our time"—we call it,
"our" time, as if we ever had
the smallest hold on it.

This disparaging voice—all a
colloquy between two invented
modes, this lonesome mood

which one clings to as a balm,
all some imbecile gesturing at
dignity, and a final barrier to love.

People in Hell are clothed
in coats and dresses, some of
the women wear lace, some

are richer than others, own
a face that possesses white
smiles. In the fashion of that

place, they all say hello
to each other. Such is Hell
in its democracy. Without

the clothes they moan and weep,
that is their fashion, too. This
takes place on Saturdays, after

the parties are through. Over
all, and through the smoke
and flames of the posters

(hung for prospective guests)
absolute horror persists. One
might think it the earth,

but that the evil insists
on being recognized. Dandy
Satan has his choice of pain.

Nothing grimmer than dawn at noon.
It is grey and not awake.
The people are all dead.

All of them too, are dead.
All the people at noon.
These streets with dull sounds.

It is itself. There: and there.
One strikes a foot against the concrete.
One's own foot.

My foot: some of the dead peer at me.
The sun shines beyond this area.
Shining on dead planets.

We do not see it.
Baudelaire was absolutely right.
All dead in this macabre geography.

A stinking city full of stinking
people. What things they do
are not flowers, but are sometimes

flowery. They know that they
are garbage and this fact
somehow consoles them. Their

faces grin from the news,
their voices, remembered, are
vomit. But there are flowers

in the sky! one shrieks. There
are flowers in the sky,
agrees another. Hearts pump

blood, long ago sold. These people
are real, are real, they are
absolutely rotten, and are real.

Where are the rose-colored cities
we dreamed of? Some croaking voice stops
in the head. In the dead

center of the heart. It is one term
of reality: a man stands outlined,
held against the dull grey cities

we have all invented. He pushes
to be seen, and to be understood.
His voice (which is prose) is

all about, not only his voice,
but about the fact that his voice
is prose. The moon is not black,

but might as well be. It is not
visible. The prose goes on, it
makes its own reality, which is:

making a place in what
we dreamed was a place
for a rose-colored

city! The place is
for a voice which
talks about a voice which talks

about its own reality. Its own
term of reality. Where are
the moonlit cities we dreamed of,

and thought of as a possible
entrance to reality? The moon may
as well be black. It is invisible.

There is no instance that was not love:
at one time
or another. The seasons move

into the past. The seasons shove
one another away, sunshine or rime—
there is no instance that was not love,

one kind or another. Rough
winds at us all now, one kind
or another. The seasons move

away from birds; jays, doves:
or they fly into them, fly, climb,
no instance that was not love.

It is not just some scent on a glove
nor a glittering coin, a dime
or another: the seasons move

unerringly, stolid and bluff.
One would like to find
one instance that was not love;
another;
        the seasons
              move—

(Sonnet with X's)

Around here's a world that we love:
familiar dullards move
through it. Hello! A groove

in a sky holds sun
which always shines—or shows dun
regardless our wants. Fun

static in *loci* like beaches.
Breasts some men reach
for, soft beneath some wretch's

mouth. There is no winning.
But a constant priming
of the pump, if the timing

is wrong one joins the wrecks.
They merely groan: their spot, an X:
X: X: X: X.

A red sun is going down somewhere
I cannot see it. I have perhaps been there.
Some girl with pimples watches it:

The long blue shadows on the hills.
The trees move imperceptibly, the falls
crack below on boulders, shit

Floats down the river. She is waiting
for her lover, the shadows staining
now her summer dress, she sits

Looking out across the river. A red sun
almost gone, September gone, a red moon
rising and the girl's sweat

Dries. She waits for her lover, black
settles on the earth. One places stock
of sorts in such projection: my pale moon sets.

A particular density: in the center, rises
and forms, making an image. Reality.
A kiss, a strong hand-

shake. A black face moving
out from the paint on either side, drawing
aside

a curtain. A face of unutterable
evil, The Valley of the Shadow
of Death: (he fell

backwards, tripping over
the cans of paint on the floor;
later, he smoked and got drunk.

His head, his brain solid, in
the center, with that black face, now
static, still, frozen peering.

A door that opens on
my world, a scene of ice, frozen
crisp, with gin:

a door closes, opens, the eye moves in-
voluntarily across the white
mirage, the harsh bright

fluid posts it, the tongue wants
this balm to move one from the haunt
grim in sunlight: reality

(A system edged with falsity,
reality is caught winds redolent
of juniper (All the drinkers went

What is to be understood:
the world, one's place
in it. The meaning of

it, the meaning of
any part of any of
it, this desk, from

wood, of wood. Quiet
forests underneath the
sky. A blue sky, a black

sky, endless. There is
a pattern, not what we choose
to make, the humiliated artist.

Come from the whirling zodiac
"circle of animals"
hoi barbaroi,

if you will, impinge
on this earth, change its
patterns of hate, the love

corrupted and soiled. *Hoi
barbaroi,* the rain of
animals, zodiac fix on

the acts, of us the servants
here of greed and error. Come
from the path of the sun

come, *barbaroi,* pour on
this earth, come, I call
on you. Fix this dirt.

Come all ye Sons of Art
out under the blue, let the
commanders gaze through

their rosy spectacles, one holds
the earth in hand and
the hand gets dirty. Let them

go off in the blue, away, O
Sons of Art, away into
a million Christmas dinners

gallons of egg nog, red
packages and blue to thrill
them (as they will be thrilled

Come away, come away sweet
Sons of Art, the sun that shines
on you is sun clear through.

L the simple shape
a song a baffle for rats
down and up a song

and to the side
a song up and down
and then to the side

L a baffle for rats
to go wrong L the letter
12th in the song

of the alphabet and L
such simple shape a baffle
for rats a tune a jape

In the blue, singa
the song, old corpses
turna to dust, the handa

gone or bones. Old
birds moult or do
something, la la singa

the song. "Man of
destiny," he say, gimme
the smoke, fucka

the world, outa the
blue, singa the song
nothin to do, alla

the people they deada
go wrong, skeletons
no singa no song.

Some hawk-nosed man
striding my old streets,
goodbye forever.

A madman with gold
rimless glasses,
so long pal.

Fat men and lean
that bitter corner,
goodbye, goodbye!

"My youth was a
darkening storm" goodbye,
sweet hearts and pals.

It is one man alone, what
other way
to say it. I am sick of myself.

My loneliness one took
for blazon.
Proud: I am tired of that.

I am a depressing
man, I write
depressing poems.

Alone, sick of myself. Summer
ain't what it
used to be, heart. Of my heart.

How I loved that melody,
a thing, it was, it was
an entity, fresco, substantial,

part of a season, color fixed
in plaster, gentle and mordant
on the air it was. The sound of it

bright over waters of the lake.
Morning. Sunlight. The water
quiet on the raft. My

body, it was, my ear, my
possibility of life, still, a fresco
it was, some melody I forget

what. A tone it was. A mix
of life and time dying
in sunlight: I loved that melody.

But the light is imagined
is it not? The best kind. An
ordinary light it was, I have made it

something superior, extra-terrestrial.
The flowers of a color ordinary
to them—or a lack of color. White:

everything in the area
of that snapshot that lived
is dead. Gnats, mosquitoes,

flies and worms—those secret
lives all dead as you are
mother. The exquisite

photograph is yellowing,
the edges curled, all those
secret lives are long, long carrion.

Mother, this is a ball of color.
Dazzling, soft, sweet. Could it be
"life"? If one should simply, choose it.

Reach for it. (Don't bother me, go
away, you say, life. Life, bull shit. Life
stops. Abrupt. Sudden. Breath. Out.

The last batter, the long shadows
out across center field, has
struck out looking. K.

(pentagram)

Who
will
remember

that past
is
past—

beyond
our wish
to

care
for it
?

(the light
frozen
forever:

the night
filled with
water

: rain.
one face
moves us

—
to love
beyond

past—
to
perfect

nostalgia.
One
face.)

CORROSIVE SUBLIMATE (1971)

One thought the recurring "image" in the poet's song an
instance of consciousness,

Clear, clear day, in sun, one's majority upon one, it
is seen to be simple obsession, and helpless,

The mind careening through the infinite spaces of itself
snags on some plain word:

Through and between whose familiar letters the true
true image of what happened: of the blank world.

In his poem the poet
is mired in embarrassment, no
propositions, neither
answers.

And no questions.
Whom he soothes
he soothes, redresses
no grievances.

Fuck the ginkgo.
I dislike mountains.
You can look out the window
and write of them proficiently
life long.

"An interesting emotional state"
that writer who can no longer
read. Other "interesting" states
wild and empty. Montana, ah.
Wyoming, Colorado, ah. Who can forget
New Mexico. Well,

Fuck the ginkgo. And do not embarrass
painters by being warmly confused.
Fail, fail, if you must but in terms
you are helpless within.

I do not like mountains. There
is bloody sun or bloody snow, mist or
gold. Then dark. Then tomorrow.

The ginkgo lends itself
to ornamental potting. Artists
I know are broken in their art
to which their bitter faith is given.

I am tired of new materials. I don't want
to read aluminum poems any more. Don't
tell me about Cuba.

All the keys shine. Locked door.
In the bare rooms within Baudelaire dead
and dead. Elegant black suit a slight

Shine to it.

I don't want to hear any news on the radio
about the weather on the weekend. Talk about that.

Once upon a time
a couple of people were alive
who were friends of mine.

The weathers, the weathers they lived in!
Christ, the sun on those Saturdays.

Rose Room

Strange memorable objects:

caught in the most elegant turn of
the mind.

> In an old stupid film
> two stars enact the unwed
> couple
>
> in a roadhouse. They dance
> alone, to white swing music
> they embrace in static
> lust.
>
> The quality of light!
> in that scene, the absolute
> smell of summer out of
> fields, the distant haze
> implied thereon, these
>
> two stars danced into
> my youthful head.

So that, later, I saw a roadhouse
in that light, and danced in one,

the girl I was with and I
moved into that gentle occasion.

(Oh turn into summer, what
quality of American light
that is not bitter

is departed

I speak now, tell you a bright truth:
This is a bitter city.
All the poets in disguise, as if
They lived here. (You can tell them,
                    they're the ones who
                    have the weary smiles
                    and laugh a lot with people
                    who don't know them.

Do you think that 20 years of wind
off the Atlantic won't change you?
                                        Wrong.
Or 30 years? 40?

When you leave this town you
Is just campin out   (thus the black porter
                        to my mother,

                        on her honeymoon.

God what a bitter word.

Land of Cotton

One remembers hysterical laughter
a summer night, when no one was happy.

Sam, come from the town, come the fire
consumes you, the trees are ablaze, the church
the money
is burning, any old photo

will prove it so.

The guernseys, the holsteins,
brahma bulls screaming in terror!

(Cold, ice cold sauternes
through all the whisky
fog, the dawn near.

  Sam, the town is burning,
your Byronic scarf
will not save you. Here, *phlox* is not
the decorative flower,

come from the town Sam, you are
burning. I call you Sam to
come, gazing at the photo where you stand

while all around you rages

Long Gone Blues

The face in the quiet night.
Absolute darkness, someone is
fishing downstream.

Words to be forgotten,
late, old stupid clothes, styles
that no longer exist.

Life. Movement of air, zephyrs,
the hit of bass or pickerel, somehow
love in it, the middle of it.

I ask you where was it, the space,
the air displaced? Gone on air?
Men dead from cannon fire and

grenades, children born, strange
lives beginning to find shape, where
is that sustenance, that past location.

Perceive

With a sudden shock
it comes to me that I am more
father

than my father was. I who
have lived so consistently
with children. But not

to say I am not my father's only son.
I am my father's only son
you do understand. He is

my father, and was father
for so long so many faithless
and ignorant years

stolid and remote
almost a placidity given,
and held, maintained certainly

in that far that dignified
location.

Poem

The clear objects
one grows to love. The clarity
of objects one gets simply used to.
A beloved child, his particularity,
old friends missing on two
cylinders.

Did someone say Baudelaire?
It is Baudelaire as well
become object to the eye and ear.
That puritan glance, the agony
of his purity of pity for himself
that was never self-pity. That stern eye.
Those elegant black suits.

To someone who said Baudelaire
I say: Baudelaire. I say
moonlight of memory. I say
blue notes.

My youth is left in the heads
of a mere clique of people
who no longer know each other.
I say grey stone to my Baudelaire.
I insist Wallace Stevens was a tragic man.
I say there are slicks of mud
and puddles on my mother's grave.
What is in my head is the remnant
of arcane formulae wrought
for their particular perfection.

Toward the End of Winter

Brought almost to tears
by the simple presence of myself
in my own flesh, in the chair,
my familiar things around

Approaching my 38th year.

Partly drunk I am returned
returned to a startling moonlight
the shadows of trees subtly
moving swift toward water
and varied perfumes, in my chair,

by an old record I thought to discard.

In its faded loveliness the loss
of the singer is in me, her
clear voice doing the stupid song
honor, now she is forgotten

as the song. Approaching my 38th year
shaken at the absolute mass of my experience
the deadly facts of it: they are endless,
filled with faces, I hear voices behind
that lost vocalist's clear words.

Though it be rejected, rejected,
approaching my 38th year I am aware
of the truth of all time lost and buried.
Every act, each careful gesture
in tableau, I see the exact blouse

and how it smoothed over a young girl's
shoulders, her sweet fat.

These clarities, moving to aromas
the singer enmeshed with the reality
of her voice in her own presence, of flesh.
Approaching my 38th year, the long dance
of each and every face, the delicate
timbre of each laugh, there is no truth
but in dead event, shaken, stunned

I miss everybody.

Marjorie

Well she walked out of my life. Her young breasts
and the glitter of hair bleached
on her thighs.

Now there must be
stretch marks beneath her fitted girdle. She is
kindly toward her husband.

I had
the very bud of her, beauty and clarity
day clear.

Hello to her hello I kiss
your palm

God all the things destroyed since I last kissed her
on what bitter corner in the Bronx.

Coast of Texas

Sur la côte du Texas
—Apollinaire

1.

Although the sky
was bright blue and clarity
the exact love

That blank city allows
at times: so that it
did not seem I was

In Hell
I was in Hell. O
love. That impairs my song.

2.

Corpus Christi
is no place to spend Christmas
notwithstanding those avenues
of palms, the white houses on the green Gulf.

The old Mexicans fish off
stone quais, and fish off stone quais.
I ate chili and drank rye whisky.
A whole novel wrote and discarded in my head.

Notwithstanding those avenues of green
palms, Corpus Christi on the coast
of Texas is no place to spend any time.
Apollinaire himself avoided this blank city.

3.

He never knew it could
be so cold in the streets
of that white city. Walks around
insane the wind tears water
from his eyes.

He thinks he sees her face
in the palm trees, love breathed
out of a bad hotel. In his madness.
His hand that touches him
is hers.

The palm trees the palm trees
are moonlight. His heart is drowned
in the Gulf. O let down
your hair you.
You blue water.

4.

In that sunny room dreamed
he lay with her, book open, his hand
on his crotch.

He woke to the bright day and
smell of weak coffee. Walking
around the room, he went walking
around the room, briskly.

Fuck this sun, O fuck this rotten sun,
O fuck this sun, O sound of gentle bluish waves
piling up. Glanced in the closet
and saw her.

5.

Here they are all running down in the night into the sea
off the Coast of Texas. Bad dreams, yellow.
He wrote stories on hotel stationery
and wept into the pillow. It serves him right
he says in someone else's voice. Dream
of fame. Well the wind
is very wet blowing out of Mexico. She
walked out of his life dragging
his heart along. In her fucking yellow blouse.

6.

A man with a battered
bluish face stands in the sun
on the dock and tells him
about books.

What books! What a vision
of America he has he says, a style
so sweet that. The young man
burning thinks of the woman he loves.

All in the burning sky
she is, all in the burning
sky. And a whiff of orange cunt
come out of Florida.

7.

The interminable novel
between the lines green eyes.

The sheets were rumpled
and he read.

God they twisted their
way through the pages.

There was one simple arrow
of a line in her voice.

Coming from the dead
center of each o.

This is a resort town,
blanco.

8.

She is almost unbearably
nubile. And when I reflect
on the place

Where her slender legs join
in absolute silk I find
myself walking

Around in circles
outside Galveston, sure that
I'll be arrested

But too out of my mind
to care, crazy
in the flash from the Gulf.

9.

Where he walked around
he wished. He could see a woman. To
take her place, to be with him
to his imagination that spare
odor.

Well.

He watched himself narrow in
the eye, a slender young figure
in a faded field
jacket.

A year later he was happy. Then
he was unhappy for a long long time.
In that wash of fearful wet air
thick in the moonlight

off the Gulf received the poet's
true guerdon.

Unhappy. A coal. A live coal
burning through and through
his life. He has given them

all what he can give them

the rest
died in a hotel room
with no radio

10.

In the pale light he sees her mouth
open and the tongue come out
in her heat.

> Nothing there but the spot
> where the road turns
> east toward Galveston.

He sees her eyes catch the light
catch the light. Over her his bare knees
in the sand.

> Two cars with Louisiana plates
> gone up toward the glow
> from some diner.

Her breasts free of her blouse
up toward his lips a small pearl
button cold against his cheek.

> To live through this
> is to live through anything. He
> shouts directly out of the
> whisky thinning his blood.

Under the streetlamp waiting
for a bus her face is
gentle in the beginning rain, that
was another seacoast. Grey water.

11.

Everyone knows Apollinaire
went mad on that hazy coast, dazed
under the blue. I went mad
there too.

  Particular articles of apparel certain
  girls should not be allowed
  to wear. Stuck in the mind.

I thought of her with the bell
ringing behind her voice. I thought
of her with the bell.

  I wrote down the precise colors
  in an old notebook lately come across.
  Scent of Castile.

No thing for a grown man
to be up to. Well, her smile
anyway was a crooked one.

  Crash and bang from bar
  to bar, fall in the water, if you
  could see my whole face suddenly

"You'd know just how I've been"

12.

The sun off the dusty palms
clumped around the Greyhound
station. He goes from the Coast of Texas
                          to another city

soon. His cigarette smoke creamy.
Fur. Long before he touched her
breasts stroked the fur collar
                          of her coat

and smelled the cool lining.
When he touched her breasts
they were clearly as he knew they were
                          cool in his hands

he looks at yellow in the sun.
No reason to leave this
white city she is walking through
                          white cold humming

a metal carol
the snow of course melting
of course on her hair
                          and fur

13.

Why have you done this? wrote
and crumpled the letter. Don't you
believe that I could have died for you?
and crumpled the letter.

   The liquor store still open but
   he had plenty of liquor, My fingers are
   cramped holding the air that is you.
   Said that.

It is impossible (I'm sorry
for me not to write, here in my blue
sport shirt in this holiday time
at least to say how much I

   He left that paper on the little desk
   and leaned his hands against the wall,
   nothing to make or tear down
   his hands on the wall. Vague and broken

14.

Matagorda, Seadrift, Corpus Christi.
Went back into time into clear cold and
a true spring. Actually smelled his fingers.

Later, he understood Lorca's despair, that
white and waxy lemon. That was his heart.
It was No.

You can squeeze it one way or
squeeze it another, smother it in the warmest
of wind

Once the blood has fallen out of it
the blood has fallen
out of it. (Kline smiling.

15.

It was cinnamon that she liked?
Liked Fidelio. Yellow skirts, bit
her nails. Under the limes
he remembered and invented memory.

A woman in a tailored suit too
warm for the day smiles at him
moving from shade to brightness under
the trees.

He smiles back, certainly licorice . . . ?
Probably sweating a little under
the arms, old enough to be his mother,
a gracious fuck. Waft of cloves.

16.

He would come back out
of this butter sun, walking the
2000 miles. Her hip leaning
against a tree her foot pointed in.

Crawl through the snow and
kiss her stockings and the collar
of her blouse. Even through Georgia.

He will listen to opera and Jewish
jokes, get the fuck down
in the slush and touch
her shoes.

Do without a hat in the wind
off the Atlantic and weep
into her crotch.

He could sleep in pajamas get up
to a job and eat lunch with
fascists and morons, buy her
boxes of Tampax.

She had a crooked smile put
his hands between her garters
and her thighs.

A Poem for My Wife

Certain figures seem to control
the mind, flame and die
flame again. The past
is minute changes in movement.
Such subtle air.

It is immediately over
but the history.

What that is: precise
taste of lemonade
in the dark field of the fair.

I can no more piece out
my amalgamation
than retrieve the red prize hat.

Old Tale

In some strange replica or congruence
of legend in sunny Europe (they know how to live!
someone in a limpid tower
may wait for me (eating crusty bread (and Camembert!

Here in New York
if she does not love me
then I am not loved.

Research, Again

In the center of a peach
there was a world that he wanted.
(A poetic fancy fancy. The peach
was brilliantly real.

(Aside, friends, he stood
at the table, his wet sponge, the
crumbs, stains from the wineglasses.

And felt the love disappear into
the air for a time.

I feel that this is right.
I feel that this is right.
I'm tired of lovers and the newly
married.

Sighing (against the smudged wall
Some baroque sanity bright there
The love comes back in as it comes
back in. No use in pushing anything.

Love, is pronounced, as
its changes are rung and discovered,
he did not say.

Pail

Puncture: this is when
those images one thought dead or
sprawled narcotized awake, awake
and with terrible precision move
into the heart. At once.

Abrasion: occurs drunk, you fall
against something sober you never would
have got even near. All the skin of
the heart, raked off, all the heart
burns.

Incision: comes out of a soft wind
and lays you bare at the moment you
are telling a really good story, with
gestures. The wind goes off down
the street with you.

Laceration: the whole organism you
thought intact turns and tries to get
out of itself while you smile and
hold it together,
the head collapsing.

Poem

Living friends live
in the past so they bore us.
Running down that old nomenclature
of lovers, who and what

we did. The dead
cannot be told anything so we revere them.
That past is static. That is a photo.

              Friends, the voices
just about through that old tale a thousandth
time, a thousandth subtlety, we listen
somewhere in Ohio (mist and corn

But mine—even the dead
sit up flaking in their graves—mine

is the heart
that fell apart
at the junction unremembered

A Poem to Read in August

We sang plenty old songs then
Let me
Tell you.

There is a moment at which you
Must know that things
That are gone

Are gone. Ah the alacrity
With which
They puncture the heart.

> In the meantime: with pussy
> willows, gladioli, narcissi,
> honeysuckle, forsythia, crocus,
> peach, plum, and cherry

Blossoms, spring comes.
Check.

The New York Times: A Poem for Ross Feld

He wanted to look in the news
to find something out
about himself. See some old face
in a perfect pose so that the voice
might come forth from it in familiar
pattern.
       Find out
he was disappointed in love or
caught many many lobsters, standing
in faded jeans and sunglasses
with some big fucking blue
marlin next to him. In the rear
the shimmering Atlantic.
              Read of his
death or his betrothal to a girl
with shining hair come out
of Massachusetts and aroma of good
cognac and fresh horseshit.
              Find something out
anyway but the rain nervous
against the window ah. A long day
and a long night and a long day
and another night and then Sunday.

Prince Rupert's Drop

Well, now he's decided to be happy.
A new suit, seen with his wife
(between girls
        at all the right spots.

They're both happy. Love sweet love
is their preoccupation. "What a bitter
man"
        G is.

They'll show us old bastards
how to write, grrr. R is
a letter of enormous
        beauty.

They have no touch with
my secret heart my source
so that in the night I
        go there while they dance.

It all devolves on what
one wants and what is happy,
no? This is not
        haiku. Fuck the ginkgo.

Baudelaire, who once explained
Mao, drunk on cognac (his
cuffs damp

    was heeded by Rimbaud:
    arrogant bourgeois
    colonist. A nance to boot.

The bird. The bird. There
was something about an
albatross, some "symbol"
they call it.

    Alexei Stakhanov and
    Horst Wessel, both, in their way,
    devoted men, thought it a "symbol."
    Did they not.

They Die Over and Over. In the Movies

Dark night, pale, spare image.
The rhythm faint
and nervous.

Wherever he looks he sees strangers
full of ambition and a sense of right.

Did he know the skies falls down?
The sky fall down? To the barbarous clangour.

What is most unusual is the pleasure
all take in the oncoming maelstrom, great

Death itself some old lover suddenly met
on the street or arrested. At the steam

table in a cheap cafeteria (that is familiar.

Blue Turning Grey

Filled here with contempt.
Of which a simplest definition: failure

to honor the beautiful and innocent.

Our filth perfectly in our eye.

The other night, old Satch hit notes
way past his prime that were perfectly

chimes. The ringing of that music
a parcel of a last belief and hope

for cleanliness.

The Insane Waiters

Gentlemen, gentlemen, these
are the waiters I mentioned in my friend's work.

(One has a bowl of soup and is caught
in simple frenzy. A hand, another, up to
the ceiling with his order pad, these

are the insane waiters.

Dozens more, raging, guffawing, the steam.
The swinging door to the kitchen where other
waiters are battered against the pots
and blistering coal stoves.
These are the waiters,
gentlemen, in my friend's work.

Discarded, torn across and thrown
to the garbagemen, they will persist,
they are the entire world before us,

supplying supplying the goods, the good

so good, good goods: terrific in their smoke
their perfectly hilarious evil.

Veterans of Foreign Wars

What makes one man go mad makes
us all mad, forgive them.
Baudelaire who distrusted his time.

Generals do their duty, do you imagine
for a moment that Grant or Pickett
would have spared the gook hamlet?

It is in our bones, no end
to it, it is a profession of
our own dearly hated ethic.

The sexual revolution is here!
(Meanwhile, and meanwhile . . .
Luxe, calme et volupté. Oh

yeah. Well, richness, calm,
and sweet sweet pleasure, driftin.
Driftin and dreamin. While

every wall falls down, sex is
the simplest act of no
moral courage or persuasion.

(General Grant drunk on his porch,
thinkin bout the good ole days, he was
simply a butcher, who knew it, or

as the blunter Spanish say,
down with intelligence. long
live Death.

See America First

One: recalling going somewhere.
America is flat out before you, they
   want to pull you into it
   or set up beers in any mill town
   They fight in the roads in the moonlight.

Two: there's the magnificent city!
A white grain elevator dazzling in the light
   White Buildings is no accidental title,
   nor the unemployed in Hagerstown.
   They'd smash your car for a nickel.

Three: into sunlight and rain O
after a while the corn is just foliage,
   Who can care about it?
   Who can care about it?
   They shoot you down in far acres.

Four: running out of gas in Arkansas
in a fantastic rainstorm:
   They have chili in one town
   made with Heinz's ketchup.
   They shit on the floor in the washroom.

If you get through you can see Sausalito.
   They fight in the roads in the moonlight!
   They'd smash your car for a nickel!
   They shoot you down in far acres!
   They shit on the floor in the washroom!

Anatomy

Certain portions of the heart
die, and are dead. They are
dead.

Cannot be exorcised or brought
to life.

Do not disturb yourself
to become whole.

They are dead, go down
in the dark and sit with them
once in a while.

SULPICIAE ELEGIDIA / ELEGIACS OF SULPICIA (1977)

1.

At last comes love of such a quality that it would shame
    me
more to weave a cloak for it than to show it naked.
Swayed by my Muse's charms, the Queen of Cythera has
    brought him
to me, folded him into the curve of my arms, my heart.
Venus has kept her promise: let my delight be recounted
by all those who have not their own delight.
I will not bury or seal up my poems to my love
to keep others from reading them before him, no.
I exult in my foolishness, to wear a face to silence gossip
sickens me: we are borne to each other, worthy of each
    other's love.

2.

My hated birthday looms. In the rude and wretched
    country
and without Cerinthus, it will be a sad occasion.
What is sweeter than the city? A country house
in Arretino, its frigid river and frozen fields?
Is this a fit place for a girl? Rest, Messalla, uncle,
you guard me much too closely. Not all trips
are good ones, and this, this one takes me away from
    Rome,
yet here I leave my senses. Your power, uncle, permits
    me none.

3.

Do you know that sad journey is lifted from your
    darling's heart?
She'll be permitted to spend her birthday here in Rome.
Let us all celebrate that day, my day, my birthday,
what good luck that I can give the day to you.

4.

That you allow yourself this vast neglect of me
—how good of you. It swiftly cures my awkward
    stumbling
after love. To follow whores, to press against
their white skins in their white wool shifts
delights you more than does your own Sulpicia:
but our friends are pained, they are vexed to see
my place, my bed, ceded to some nameless slut.

5.

Cerinthus, don't you have some soft thought for your
       girl
now that fever tortures her shivering body?
I don't want to recover, to survive this morbid illness
unless you also want me to.
What good is it to get well when you,
in your iron heart, feel nothing for me?

6.

Light, my light, let me never be again
the flaming love I was, I think I was to you
just a few days ago, if I don't bitterly regret,
more than any foolish thing my youth has done,
leaving you alone last night. I thought to mask
the flame that flames in me.

WHITE SAIL (1977)

Boilermakers

Rich and poor
of every color and idea
show themselves
mannequin and dummy.

Who must apologize
for tatters
of integrity?

In purple light with
the dream quality of honey.

Cynical

Here is a curious picture
of young maniacs dragging
their madness into the woods.

We are all going mad perhaps.
"Lead in the air" one says, a rich
man costumed like a maharajah
bored in Nantucket.

You recall the People? They
may be defined as any two animals
whose greed meshes in time.

In any city park you may
descry citizens of Mars also
incognito, speaking tin pizza
and white port.

A Silk Ascot for the Terrorist

A time
all beliefs or loved things
are fashion or are not.

The young convinced by
the most heartless men
to buy—what? To buy

—enormous packages
of ways to be alive. So that
they may feel alive.

The secret is
it all died 40 years ago.
Who listens to anyone?

Lacked a live replacement
so filled the land with
bitter laughter.

There is a given point
at which mockery
asks to be paid.

It ends with the painter
whose images are broken and broken
again by the addition of whites
whites whites.

With the poet whose
love's handkerchief
seems to him greater
than the world.

Think of a man in an ice-cream suit
and spotless Borsalino emerging snowy
from the hold
of a tanker.

Fragments of white. Of white
of white all that there is
to content
fragile and exact.

Captain Marvell

Naming the trees. Aromatic
summer nights, with fireflies.
Any car at all humming
through it.

Old songs persist in some
dense block of time, flying
outward to the limits
of time.

In brilliant blue. To the end
of time. We are stretched
under the chilly trees, sound
of the miniature falls.

As a tableau, flying outward
a full scene, lovers and nameless
faces, the living and dead
in glimmering blue light.

What is trapped in the brain
out at the edge of the farthest
galaxy. Looking back
at 1949: Packards and broken hearts.

Indigo hue. Brilliant azure
flash. In the morning sky,
Venus, another old ballad,
malign and sinister planet.

Lost in the Stars

What of the diary
or journal dense
with notes on planets
and stars?

It looks like explanation
or an indication
of how things will go
or be resolved.

The Arkansas cloudburst
Red water washing away
green crayoned Venus red
crayoned Mars.

Whatever lambent purl is used
for border, out beyond time
some boot, inviolate, choked
with rusty mud in a silent field.

Beautiful Soup

Heed the story of the man
who took the garbage out
and threw himself away.

A lot of smiling faces
from which come disclaimers
of guilt.

They smile, they smile.
A congeries
of famous lemons.

It is obvious that one's best
is none too good.
Whereupon a smile again.

Mosquitoes in New Jersey

Someone like I
across the pale water
in white light, smell of
flowers.

Silent smile of
recognition. Hello there.
20-year-old styles. It is
clear I is dead.

Revivify! Revivify!
The hero moves off down
the dirt road past the
weedgrown tennis court.

His heart a red light
blinking the news
in the moonglow
of an obscure accident.

George C. Tilyou Smiles

Wept to say it.
Mother of God. Tears
rolling unlike rivers rolling.

Taste of the lost waters
in which his childhood foundered.
These are remembered things. Items.

"We are not at the present time
prepared to buy the inside
of your head."

The urchin's question always was:
what if a wave a tidal wave?

The Ambassador

It might have been white paint
splattered on something black.
"Something," the man says.

Instead it was a cruel item.
A face in a bourbon dream dreamed
in sweat in a roomette.

Outside the awful banal scenery.
How it clattered by!
He glimpsed one Mexicali rose.

Years later I entered Penn Station.
How natty he was in suntans and black jacket.
Memory, as New York, froze.

Oleo Strut

Blood a rarest oil
secret in this hot machine.

The ceaseless landings
the meadows, beaches

sudden bumps and shocks
loud slams: these hopeless

cities dying in their glamour.
It is not that the body

is unaffected, but that the
heart, the dark heart

takes so much so
quietly.

Broken hearts even function on
till the body shakes itself apart.

Gimlet

Of course it is all twisted.
Lost in the miles of blood
flowing flowing from one
"vital organ" to another.
And here it is in the brain.

One speaks of one's life.
A quarter smashed flat
on a trolley track
dim in memory past Ulmer Park.
Ragged boys off to Coney.

What is it that I need?
Have I died that something
should exist to bring me back
to life? If this isn't love.
I have tried to live with some grace.

Let everyone I love forgive me.
Allow me to despise luxuriously
those I despise. The blood, the
blood. Blind messenger of error.
Let me, even twisted, touch.

You Are My Heart's Bouquet

Nobody dies of love
or of a broken heart thus
are old songs proved.

They can cause death many ways
however. Recall the blues
in which the blues in which.

Ah the silences that grow
out of exact revelations
of contempt. I have heard them.

Only love can cause them
and other instances
of the maladroit.

Prescriptions: adultery,
art, hobbies, tears, and sugar
mixed with turpentine.

"Sweet as the showers of rain"
lifts the lyric. Love lives
forever any way you see it.

Showers of rain. It is memory
puts that old foot in front of
that other old foot. Selah.

Let's Call This

Time for a toting up of concessions:
to love
or the fury for its benison.
Personally
I can go back to the thirties.

No long stories please
about maintenance of ego. God
the scattered creatures
we survive as.

The few things that are real persist
and are resurrected: on the other hand

those that rot in the ground
those that rot in the ground

ah carry flowers through the April mud
for them. Handsome cadavers.

I wish that what looked true
was true. That the rainbow sliding
over the island from the bay swept
in all its beauty all the way
to Normandy.

Say the young man among
the famous crackling leaves
of autumn walks. They are yellow
red bronze and so forth.

On his cheek a crystal in his eye
a pearl. In the dark brown
of his eye there smolders
summertime in Florida.

If you want him take him.
This is a poem about color.
This is a poem about giving people
what they do not want.

On the poet's wall a poet
stark in black and white
is falling or leaping
from a broken stool.

In his hand a secret text
from which he reads the past
out of the present. One might call
the book *The Blues.* Or not.

In one poem a young man
scuffles through the crunchy leaves
of fall. He just got a haircut.
Last night he felt a thrill.

Ages ago. Last night. What night
does this madman speak of? Who writes
the hidden poem about whom? Text
of color. O soft rose of dawn.

Charles and Arthur

Pieces of that steel
seen regularly give
the stomach its persistent ache:

it has been a tragic time
for everyone forever.

The steel in terrible configuration
that has no answers
save that the earth is diseased.

A bitter faith in men
by slow degrees destroyed: God is dumb.

We wish the stern design
to glitter to entertain we make it
into fountains of spun platinum.

Men prove their love for one
another by just slaughter.

The skies are azure: peace
a cheap boutonniere: yet and yet
this terrible metal

This terrible metal
says goodbye
for all of us.

Deluxe Assorted

Now in the turnings of the poem
I will that Hart Crane once again
leap into that platinum ocean
so my words may strut for him.

The label on the bathrobe
reads *Macy's Herald Square.* He raises
his hand from out the sparkling
wash of turquoise.

His sea is left: past rhetoric
past idea and mystical abstraction.
Certain purities that are rooted
and quite unassailable.

Out of the broken world into
the diamond-studded waters and down.
Some passengers fleck the rail
as he shyly waves from the tinsel.

Drunk again. Goodbye cider,
goodbuy Ohio, so long.
He vanishes the ocean spanking
bright blue candy wrapper.

Blackburn's Dream

In the dead man's dream I stood
a priest. Turning from the altar
a catcher's mitt of thorns

on my hand. This message from Provence
where they know such *vidas*.
Rest, rest unworldly friend.

That dreams are nonsense
creates in them flat terror.
I saw a porch.

Women all in black. My boyhood
friend's mother with his face.
She fainted at my mother's corpse.

All my fanatic labor has earned me
less than a thief. The dead are dead
forever. Dim rays. Darkness.

Rest, sweet friend, unworldly mother.
What is there to say? At 46
I cannot fix this life that hurt you.

Billy McCoy

Looking in my poem, I see myself.
Not mirrored, myself, mark,
at a desk.

Myself. Keep the reflection
device where it is most at ease
with those casual letters
to old friends in Tulsa and Akron.

Mark of myself in the poem.
Not what I seem but myself.
So that the poem's true intent be seen.

So that the poem's true intent shine forth.

Mark of, ah God,
the true poet.

September in Kittery

Those were the lobsters
many poets write of, compare
to us and our lives: blindly
crawling, dark in the dark.

      Whereas I write: vanilla, then
      lavender, then—anything.

What is there to compare
with what? Here is sun the snow
is melting. Here a crow
of memory. Old Valentines.

      Priests who were afraid and
      those who drank too much.

Bad wine, blended whisky, the special
on beer. A white sail
on the Sound off Connecticut, breathless!
Ask the maniac, Artaud.

A Hit Album

The bride the groom the small grin
on the flower girl. The boy
in his velvet suit
has wet his pants. Dim light
of tragedy.

Not even tragedy
but the winding down the tons
and tons of minutes filled with Labor Days
line drives bacon and eggs
over easy.

Sunny sides. They showed their
sunny sides. Not all of them with
perfect teeth. They did their best.
The ugly too. That they died
without banners.

It's terrific. Steeped in innocence
or remorse the wondrous faces
in the photographs. O dearest God
some pity for these briefest smiles.
Rain and silence.

THE ORANGERY (1978)

1939 World's Fair

I still hear those azure carillons
floating from the Belgium building
caroming off the Trylon

and the Perisphere. Magic land.
Herr Dreyer grumbled because there was no
swastika. In "Florida" fake orange trees.

    My mother was beautiful
    in the blue gloom.
    How she loved me.

    Sore feet and headaches
    Depression and loneliness
    dulled her soft bloom.

She died ice-grey in Jersey City
with no solitary word.

Everybody would soon change
or die. Sudden burst
of my mother's youth revealed
when I was ten.

Thin dreams of my "new life"—
gone, gone. Thank God
all dreams are rubbish.
If they were not? A smell of rose oil.

I see her clear in a white dress
dear woman. The mist on Jersey fields.

Potato chips and orange drink
in the cool taproom
of the Warren House
thrilling summer afternoons.

She whom no one ever found
death found in Jersey City.

Monsieur Mort, in a stupid play
is a Frenchman of perfect grace.
Politely he refuses orange ice
with vanilla ice cream crowning it.

He prefers crème glacée, eh? He
smoketh Gauloises and Gitanes.

In the "film" they make of it
the plot is slightly warped.
Still, the gent simpers on and on
about his business. You know.

All in black with a French accent.
Plenty of crackling wit.

Chez Macadam

The building had better days.
Immured in a situation "symbolized"
by orange.
I mean, it saw better days.

God only knows
what the rest of us saw. I know
what I saw. There was
certainly a roadhouse or two.

Off the highway orange drink
and cool Maria Elena. Afternoon
stilled in a smile
and a current pop tune.

I have decided this in the last minute.
It is as true as true.

Mr. America last seen crossing the road
in a cloud of Rum and Maple smoke.

His hair gives off the scent of eau de Rose
and the late sun finds out his white shoes.

His burnt-orange slack suit glows
with an elegance precisely mellow.

A woman in a dress a spanking white
releases an enamel smile.

She has a white rose in her teeth no guile
flickers in her wide azure eyes.

Her hair is blond she dies she dies
inside for love for love has died.

He boards the train in cindery smoke.
The sun the color of her dress now. White.

Across this water sits a shore
patched together out of dim and smudgy colors.
It brings to mind a cartoon oddly porous.
Static on a worn-out sponge. Yet a core
of translucent light seems to spring
from the center of what looks a town or market
and drenches the lime-green haze of the park
I put there. One seesaw, one fountain, and one swing.

Mothers and children in blue
filled with good humor, china blue
eyes and the rest, plus the sky is blue.

You can see I'm trying to get there
seriously. When I get there
I'll be young again. I forgot orange. There.

Canta Naranja

The sweet of dreams
is a Mexican Hat.
The sweet of dreams
a sombrero.
A sweet of dreams
on the street of dreams.
  Canta no lloro.

The sweet of dreams
is an orange hat.
The sweet of dreams
has vanillo.
One dreams of the sweet
on the street of dreams.
  Ay! Ay! Perdido.

The pale moon sails out blank.
Green fruit in the trees and
in the green trees oranges.
They are limes they

are oranges. The n is a kind
of fly that lands on
nothing. The birds flash
in morning silver light.

Glitter and buzz of.
the transparent.
flash of green.

handful of silver coins
caught by the girl the
comedienne, Madame Mystère.

Variations 3

She had on a sweet vermillion gown,
Sue, the strange comedienne.
Everyone loved her, why,
even the birds sang for joy
when she swallowed the orange.

Her routine with the wax orange
was a spectacle of utter joy.
How she did it and why,
well, the queen comedienne
just smiled and smoothed her gown.

Sue, sweet Sue, a gracious interview
given to loving cameras. She was swank
and svelte and answered the questions
thus: blankety blank blank blank.

In Memoriam P. B.

Lavender, vanilla, anything.
The belt worn with such elegance
by the Mydas fly.

How still. How still.
Dusk ever. The rosy bridge.
Everything is almost perfect
In its name.

I give you the coronet, dead man.
Wear it in health. I never dream of you.
Vanilla. Orange ice. Un sombrero.
A lavish sunset soaks Brooklyn
With excruciating love.

Kings. Kings. Kings. Kings.

Ah! The streets of dream

Deux Morceaux en Forme de Banane

Bluebonnets in Texas in a cold spring.
The sky over them as blue as blue.
In a small arroyo near San Antone
a Spaniard builds a limetree fire.
This man comes from Amarillo
which exists in pale orange light
luminous in the thin blue air.

He sings: I heard the blue bells
of Sevilla banging the yellow air
ay! ay! The air in Amarillo
is not yellow but is blue. The blaze
bursts high in a cracking orange flame.
A blue Buick passes by in dusty clouds
and a blonde therein laughs toward Laredo.

Drifting South

Straight down from Amarillo
rattled Betsy Pink and Mexicali Rose
in an (past mesquite and stunted willow)
   old black Ford
they stopped for icy orangeade
and sensuously dawdled in the shade
while sunlight shimmered on their sheerest hose.

Their summer frocks were palest lime and yellow
and bored Parisienne manquée their pose
as they clattered off in their mellow
   old black Ford
bleached Paint Rock was bitterly dismayed
as señoritas stopped but never stayed
the dust and grit but rose and rose and rose.

Big Brown Eyes

Protestants often live beneath
the ginkgo tree says Mexicali Rose
with her absolute logic.

Mexicali Rose lives in Texas
where there are no ginkgos
where there are palms and limes.

Rose has some smile! And when
she cries it stays right there.
The President wrote her once.

The note went Rose O Rose
you are sweet you are fair
send me a carton of limes

send me an orange star send me
a lock of your ebony hair.

Sappho in Paris

Paris moon-drowned streets and the chestnuts blooming
silver thighs aglow and black eyes are drunken
limes and roses flash they are blue and mauve here
    oranges glowing.

Alabama Nights the café with green wine
welcomes foreign flesh "la chanteuse Lingerie"
croons "bip boom boom boom" in her silks and laces
    orchestra blowing.

Now the yellow gloom of the cave gets brighter
tables groan the tone of a sigh is lucent
golden gin with mint is the drink preferred by
    Madame Mystèro.

Soon that tropical lady tells of doomed love
    platinum starlight.

Annie from Miami

In Paris where the rue de la Nuit
meets the gold of the day
there is a small café La Vie en Rose
all of whose red-and-white tablecloths
have vases holding tiny roses

A woman with green eyes
in a black silk dress
often sips a bock there
and when I pass beneath the chestnuts
our eyes embrace in French

As this woman is Floridian
her hair is a glowing orange
I take an orange from my jacket pocket
the lady and I trade white smiles

The King of the dark tower is a lug.
Although we like your book we have
no money. Have a drink? Dinner?

Dinner is duelos y quebrantos.
Although I grow more remote I stay
out of the ivory tower.

The angels in the sky the angels
hover just outside my tower hover
in placid gusts from Miami Beach.

They know where their bread is buttered
and why not? Are they not for the most
part manes? Sweet faces and milk songs.

Duelos y quebrantos? Is this the same city
Diamond Jim's apéritif was a gallon of o. j.?

Vapid Transit

They hauled him many times
from place to place
the black locomotives of the Erie

and the Delaware Lackawanna
and Western, the diesels
of the Penn and Santa Fe.

Why he went and where he got
bathed in a haze now.

Surely there was something
some duty or a bright smile?

Orange glare on the snow
outside Needles. Cinders
and mosquitoes in New Jersey.
Cold grey walls of Joliet.

At twenty love disintegrates
with perfect ease. The phone
said no a letter no her knees
and mouth blurred.

When the rain lashed at the windows
all stupid songs seemed mysteries
and innocent items coats and rings
glowed with misery. In every city
the wind discovered me and in every wind
the burden of an idiot song.

I carried the pieces
I could find into many
an orange sunset even into
Baltimore and Waco.

She was all in black. A statement
to take its place in "The History of Ideas."

We know black here in America.
Why, it's a scream.

Stick a point of orange in it
just for fun. Just to see what comes of it.

After which: Prove that the light
of bowling alleys is romantic.
Is the very gravy of romance.
"The crème!" yells a voice.

Then, years later, drones the comic,
I recall standing on a corner
in the Bronx waiting for a bus.
Yes, yes. Waiting for a bus.

Simplicity

Once when we were younger
fifteen years ago I in tie
and jacket you in a black dress
we took the wrong train

and had to run in a cruel
sun flaming reddish orange
for the right train on
another platform sweating

with luggage and I had
a bag of pots and pans. You
seemed miles in front of me
and I ran clanging. Wait!

Now we know this
and no one else knows anything.

Canzone

On the tropical coast of Java
Arthur Rimbaud watched movies
an odd sight in his bluchers
and his orange sombrero.

He said: An excellent jelly: guava?
to an audience of weary floozies
con men thieves and moochers.
He snapped the brim of his sombrero.

He wrote: This island once was lava
to Jeans Pierres and Suzies.
Four were drunks, two butchers.
Sun glanced off his sombrero.

He returned sans medals lucre
or poetry. Lost his sombrero.

Marvellous

Certain odd emblems are needed
to freshen the spirits. This
was delivered with no tone

one grey afternoon by a man
on a corner in the Bronx.
He had a wax nose, baggy

pants. Je dis: une fleur!
a man said, the words thin
in cold vapor. Flowers

remind me of funeral homes
Raymond Banal off from work
moonlighted. Then, the comic

said, What about some Oranges?
Golden Lamps in a green Night?

White Lemons

The rich man wanted breakfast.
He wanted coffee eggs bacon kippers
orange juice.

People in such situations are
not pitiable no matter how they
shout and bang the silver servers.

Big-breasted dowagers in comic strips
say in the face of this "My dear." That's
what they say: "My dear."

We all want that breakfast some time.
Even Lorca though he disguised his oranges
as lemons almost white.

Let him crash the silver for eternity.
Who? Him. Him? Who him? White lemons?

Homage to Arnaut

Black, ice-grey, white, azure, orange,
cities, clinics, snows, and saxophones.

There are certain birds in backyards
whose chirps and cries I never liked.

Poor dandelions too and daisies,
black-eyed Susans, Queen Anne's lace.

The clarinet soft from out the roses
pitched clear nodes, rhodōnia.

Clutter of flowers I proffer to
clutter of colors, yet save one.

The magic flower whose fruit is love
l'absente de tous bouquets

And whose seed is joy whose scent
destroys ennui.

Zukofsky

Who
was that who
saw
his father
in
his shorts,
mother laughing?

Who
decided on
the
pattern?
Of
oranges?
On white.

Who was that?
Who
saw his father?
In his shorts!
Mother
laughing.
Who?

Who
decided?
On the
pattern of
oranges
on
white.

Broadway! Broadway!

Halloween is black and orange.
A song, as in "le clarinet du marmalade."
Some are happiest drowned
in a saxophone solo.

"Le jazz hot" rhymes à la Mallarmé
with tabasco: *vide* Bunk Johnson
astomp in New Iberia.

I saw Dexter Gordon play to six people
in a frayed suit. His golden horn had lost
its sheen. The notes gleamed.

Dexter in his brilliance.
Exquisite phrasing and perfect comedy.
A black velvet an
orange corona corona.

Remember the story of Columbus and the orange?
He impressed Isabella with a demonstration.
King Ferdinand thought it a sensation.
But nothing rhymes with orange.

I saw him turning that fruit in his hand
So that the whole globe, seas and all, was orange.
Now the only thing that's orange
Seems the bloody North of Ireland.

With nothing up my sleeve I rhyme with orange.
Note well the swift flutter of the letters.
As in: "There once lay a lady of letters."
With nothing in my head I rhyme with orange.

The image "clarinet marmalade" is black and orange.
Auditor dixit: "A poem! Not this boring orange!"

The Oranges Returned

In a disingenuous letter
sent from a quiet snowy place
an old friend asks why I returned
   a gift of oranges.

I am too old to answer such questions.
Even the words sat numb. His was always
a brilliant mind yet he asks about
   his gift of oranges.

I put him in a poem once. God knows
he's had his slow shock in the mirror.
Perhaps it was that grey head sent
   the gift of oranges.

It is a maniac time, friends cast about
to touch. To reawaken. Meaningless gifts.

Je Connai Gens de Toutes Sortes

I know a lot of people who once seemed
fluid, one looked and saw them trying
to find a face and pose and freeze it.
Accessories to each other's surrender.

They had tics they had habits they knew
odd things about odd things, how they
misunderstood each other. They thought
the world a place to dance in.

When I see them as seldom as I can
they speak a perfect English that is
perfectly opaque: orange sled, Swiss
chard, gin in a jar, peachblow.

They are alive with old wives or new
pieces of them strewn across the city.

Vision of the City from a Window

A high blue sky clicks into place
soon after dawn. As usual millions
live and die beneath it.

Among them comics and comediennes
those who die for a laugh
but not for laughs. Enormous waste
seems to occur and reoccur.

As I grow older many of them persist
as ghosts encapsulate in persistent
scenes dreamy yet exact.

I see them all ugly smiles
or beloved smiles as they were
in snow in trolleys in new suits
as children eating orange ice.

Fragments of an Old Song 1

On the side of a road in Alabama
an old Ford parked
the passengers here and there
in a field of white—

These people arrested
have only their surfaces
to present yet they are clear
as characters in—

Here and there in the field
in the pale moonlight a man
a woman two children
stilled in a drama that—

They are eating something.
Oranges. In a kind of beaten glamour.

Fragments of an Old Song 2

No one could enter those vast fields
of snowy cotton but the elect.

In the cascades of moonlight
they performed their rites.

There were kisses and whispered words
on the Alabama breeze.
In this candor another candor
of private mysteries.

The subtleties of magnolia
and honeysuckle of orange blossoms
borne on the air from
the south. Hammered by the light.

Their hearts careened with the falling
stars falling in glamorous silence.

Pastorale

The rushing darkness of the summer evening.
Across the dirt road from the white farmhouse
a white wooden church its yard overgrown
with sweet grasses and in the dark blue air
the slow scribbling of the fireflies.
An old black Ford with stained grey seats
parked in the massing shadows the shadows
of two horses merge in a field of rye.
In an orange light in the dining room
a woman clears the supper dishes from the table.
Sweet voices of girls from the church steps
and muffled from inside the Ford thin
popular song resplendent with half-truths
and darkness, summer evening rushing.

The Crown

1.

The smoke of an orange corona corona
releases the imagination so that
it lights upon that shady porch
on which white rockers gleam whiter
in the cool blue shadows and a woman
in orange slacks turns her head her face
composed but distant distant and you see
she doesn't know you her imagination dwells
on brown wavy hair and the scent of rose oil
departed.

Now the sunlight is compact in an orange ball
and she is alone there rocking rocking
O God! she murmurs to the emptiness.
Stares past lime trees past the orange glare.

2.

Stares past lime trees past the orange glare
into a garden. The comic sees a woman there
move amid spangles of red blue green
and orange light.

She tends her roses and her oranges
yet she is crying bitterly. He doffs
his orange hat and croons "Mexicali Rose"
yet she continues crying.

Do you remember, he says, our trip
to Florida? You were in a black dress
and we almost missed the train? I know.
I remember. No one else knows anything!

The lady feels a waft of that past glamour
the faint orange wash of thrilling voyages.

3.

The faint orange wash of thrilling voyages
had no possibility of existing
for my mother, striking in a white dress.

It was substituted for by azure carillons
chiming in the borough of Queens
of Depression and of coming war.

In her eyes the plea: Send me an orange star
went of course unheeded. This iron world
had forgotten all her photographs.

My concern was with vanilla and with orange ice
with the fake orange trees of "Florida."
With a Lincoln Zephyr the color of limeade.

She died ice-grey and silently in Jersey City
in February long before the orange twilight.

4.

In February long before the orange twilight
slathers an orange glare on the snow

dreams of Kansas possess him. He sees
in those dead white fields a woman

whose hair is a glowing orange
in a black silk dress impervious

to the bitter winds. She smiles
in French a white French smile

and unpacks a small embroidered bag
of tricks. She is the famed

Madame Mystère! late of Paris
by way of Emporia and points east.

He walks to her his brain an irregular verb.
La Mystère shakes up some Orange Blossoms.

5.

La Mystère shakes up some Orange Blossoms
places them on the table with a little jar
of honey and a bag of pots and pans.
Perhaps she does deserve the jeering.
Yet no one else certainly knows anything.
I mean: what do they know of magic
in Emporia or Amarillo?

Then Sue in her vermillion gown
comes on stage unwinding opaque jokes
and the room is stilled: some think of
orange sleds, some green nights, some marmalade.
A clarinet is playing and the past arrives
costumed as the spectre of a bum. Sue cracks:
"He is immured in a situation symbolized by orange."

6.

He is immured in a situation symbolized by orange.
No thrust will free him of it now, he knows.
He feels his heart to be the orange from Persia.
In summer, long ago, shooting stars
trailed platinum roaring toward Dixie.
    No one else knows anything, my love
    only we say "zeppelin."

Do you recall my clanging run
in the heat of July? my Wait?
the reddish orange of the cruel sun?
Where are my tie and jacket? your black dress?
My dear, no one else knows anything
    but we know this:
    Nothing is the thing that rhymes with orange.

7.

Nothing is the thing that rhymes with orange.
Who knows it knows it even in Laredo.
And in Laredo church bells chime and chime
until the brain surrenders.

There the blonde in the Buick went
to murmur of acceleration
and orange twilight over Joliet.

How is it that I have come out here
where nothing rhymes with orange?
I have your photo in a black silk dress
wherein your face is mystery.

These images persist snow crystals
brilliant upon this iron world. Your face within
the smoke of an orange corona. Corona.

NEW POEMS (1978–1980)

Huge Man in Tight Pants

Huff! Kitchen matches. Puff! Kitchen matches.
Various patches on the tight tight pants.
The stuff of tragicomedy with vest
For casual and sporty weekends in the country.

In the country there are casual and patchy trees
This big man sets on fire with his matches.
Various patches on his tight tight pants.

On the map of Brooklyn there are bright green patches
That are cemeteries crowded with decaying trees
Not to mention many bones to which we all will
come.

His white heavy finger falls upon the map
And he huffs and puffs and splits his pants
His vest his finger tip bright green.
In the country fires on the patios.

Some Sap Sings a Poor Pantoum

They gave her a whip and colander
Beneath the thin magnolia sky
God knows what to think of that
The fly is the Devil's mutt.

Beneath the thin magnolia sky
Alabama chokes in white
The fly is the Devil's mutt
And loves that grisly light.

Alabama chokes in white
Florida burns blue-yellow
And loves that grisly light
The color of stars and bars.

Florida burns blue-yellow
She fled there poor dear Pru
The color of stars and bars
Aglow in her underwear.

She fled there poor dear Pru
In the spas of posh Orlando
Aglow in her underwear
She tamed all the alligators.

In the spas of posh Orlando
They gave her a whip and colander
Aglow in her underwear
God knows what to think of that.

Waltz of the Empty Roadhouse

Beautiful Berta aboard a bewildering barque
Broken and blue, busted, becalmed.

So, she sadly scans the thundering thalassa
Hugely heliotrope in hue.

Brown in the brisk breeze her breasts are bright and
      bronze
Brilliantly bruised by bum's boca.

Sadly she scans, so, the thundering thalassa
Hugely heliotrope in hue.

Bereft, benumbed, betrayed by the boys of el Bronx
Brandy and blackberries bore her.

So sadly she scans the thundering thalassa
Huge, y heliotrope in hue.

Man in Old Blue Suit at the Plaza

Of pearl light and blue shadows
  Reflected by the dinner ring
  Spidery silver filigree
  And the Canal Street touch
  In the box's dark blue velvet.

What blue songs inhere
  The arias of dumbwaiters
  Melodies of gone New Jersey
  Three Guernseys in the dusk
  The facets glint clean blue.

Blue stories of girls who did it
  Plots of lingerie and heels
  Each wore her dirty monicker
  Against the antiphon of Mom
  Blue-white stones their snapshots.

Of the dead blue hands that wore it
  The wet green of Holy Cross
  This picture goes with this and this
  How sudden the clap of darkness
  The black and blue of the past

Many blue midnights ragged facts
  In the box's dark blue velvet
  The facets glint clean blue
  Blue-white stones their snapshots
  The black and blue of the past.

Última Despedida del Príncipe Poniatowski de Su Familia

I am he who writes of the Prince of faded colors
Though there are better things to do, like smoke.
I see the subtle patina of despair
Of that face despite his sure moustache.
Death must be icy blue and Atlantic grey
For those brittle shades have settled in his eyes.

Poniatowski blinks and blinks his frozen eyes
To startle off those frigid wintry colors.
Through his irises his thoughts peer out all grey.
Why doesn't he ignore the blood and smoke
And sobs and corpses and just trim his swell moustache?
He has been sent that horrifying bill, despair.

The nuns told him Judas in violet despair
Hanged himself and swayed there with his staring eyes.
The Prince quakes and gags and pulls his royal
    moustache.
Death is strolling through the fields of autumn colors.
P. lights a Lucky Strike and in the pearly smoke
Sees that leafless tree sees Judas dirty grey.

I'm a Prince, not a guttersnipe in dirty grey!
He cries, You know what you can do with your despair!
But Hell keeps manufacturing its smoke.
On his honeymoon the Prince's bride had eyes
That glittered with champagne and cognac colors
As he rummaged in her flesh with his moustache.

Now he feels a hatred for his trite moustache
And for his hair, less black than sickly grey.
He is but the Prince of wishy-washy colors
Whimpering and crying a banal despair
And damning God, his wounds, his miracles, his eyes.
Death slides toward him, a precise and silent smoke.

An interesting fact is that Death doesn't smoke
Nor does he wear a beard or a moustache.
We know that scarlet is the color of his eyes
And that his lips and tongue and teeth are grey.
These data may be found under "Death" and / or
    "Despair"
Compiled by the Institute of Dying Colors.

Suddenly the smoke becomes a man in Oxford grey
He mocks the Prince's moustache and exhales despair
Deep in his eyes gleam odd barbaric colors.

Impromptu Solo on a Balcony

Messages spelled out in stars
Bright points of someone else's daylight
Write themselves past Venus and past Mars
But Mr. Blank cannot translate them right
Messages spelled out in stars

The balcony coal-black the chump alone
Leafs through his mind's huge trash
Creased photographs sad notes a bone
A letter scrawled about some distant crash
The balcony coal-black the chump alone

The lump of coal that hurts him is his heart
Small hurricanes crash through his brain
Our inventor cannot make a part
To fix the valve that regulates his pain
The lump of coal that hurts him is his heart

An odd and spidery foreign constellation
Flickers out a note to "Mr. Mud"
Señor Blanco reads the salutation
Which seems to be in Greek and signed in blood
An odd and spidery foreign constellation

He doesn't know and yet he knows
The letter surely deals with waste and loss
The night grows blacker and his nausea grows
Are all the stars irreparable dross
He doesn't know and yet he knows

When he reaches out he touches nothing
Mr. Blanco's heart is frozen coal
When he reaches out he touches nothing
The stars crash toward the inky pole
When he reaches out he touches nothing

Jaime Valeroso y Borracho Consults His Journal

In Villa Acuña where the luna bright
sends odd shimmers through this booze
every caballero cries tequila!
the drunks spill mezcal on their clothes.

O la luna shimmers bright in Villa Acuña
and turns each caballero slightly odd
they guzzle their tequila and mezcal
this booze makes everybody everybody's pard.

Love's the gusano in the bottle of mezcal
the dead and pickled emblem of bright Venus
a plastered madam in the light of luna
tequila helps her to remove her clothes.

Drunken Villa Acuña where the ladies guzzle
pickled they turn bright and shimmer
"encantada!" they drool through their booze
rapt in their cactus-juice glamour.

The clout of mezcal its odd wormy charm
the caballeros who cry in their booze
Ah! Villa Acuña de Tequila! Bright bones
beneath the dying flesh click "encantada!"

And Venus pie-eyed in the odd glow of la luna
And caballeros plastered in the wormy night
O the odd glow of la luna
O the wormy night.

Woman Irritable because of Her Menses

Often dreaming on juicy fat tomatoes
there is the taste of garnet in the mouth

Bibi Vermillion thinks this thought right through
a haze of powder color of a twilight blush

"Solitaire without the hearts
and diamonds is a game for saps"

Miss V. eats the slimy tapioca
of a Chinese apple and then gargles port

When she was a cheap tart in Perth Amboy
Red Boob her pimp fed her only guinea red

She can't believe those two dumb cardinals
don't come from Hong Kong or Taiwan

But they are real the both of them
one is Ruby and the other is My Dear

This intelligence she gleans from the margins
of her book *The Scarlet Pimpernel*

She splits the clubs and spades and makes half
her hearts and diamonds what a girl

That's no blush but the faint pink of anger
when she sees Bud Chili ogling her knees

In Perth Amboy the nights fell to their knees
and Bibi stared into her emptiness

The evening breeze caressed the tease
Has anybody seen her pearl? Poor girl

Girl at Sixteen with Lightning

The flash of lightning and we see enameled
sitting in a chair her knees together
Joanne Fulmine from Academy St. Clare
shy and perfect in her uniform

O the despair of adolescent boys is mammoth
can she know they worship her in navy blue
they sauté themselves in blasphemy in envy
of enameled Jesus at her dazzling throat

The austerities of Latin and geometry
have not made her angular or cold
the sound her silk knees make in crossing them
the softness and the sweetness of gelato

The brief clarity of lightning does her justice
she is cut from blue silk in white light
in the dark untouched by its sudden dazzle
despairing boys implore St. Clare

It is her thoughtless grace moons of her fingernails
the body enameled to perfection in its blue
how that serge touches her cool knees
as shyly perfect she pulls down her hem

O the way she holds her ice-cream cone
the way the cream enamels her silk lips

Le Bateau d'Amour Descried on the Briny

Great ruin of the face of Paul Verlaine
graces the ensign snapped taut in the wind
the glitter and pomp of ladies
and beaux upon the decks

The light that skids across the Yellow Sea
will soon falter over Peking

Heaving and creaking through the aqua waves
on the way to kisses and despair
to Shanghai and Foochow ah what humid eyes
and lying words all delicate cuisine

The light that skids across the Yellow Sea
will soon falter over Peking

The ladies and their spangled gentlemen
from Terre Haute and Queens from Santa Fe
talking ah so carefully so sweet
that their hearts may stay intact

The light that skids across the Yellow Sea
will soon falter over Peking

It is that dissembling light that fascinates
that they find reflected in each other's eyes
fine eyes peering for the clarity
glimpsed near Cathay ten thousand years ago

The light that skids across the Yellow Sea
will soon falter over Peking

Rudderman! hold the course for Hong Kong
the slick swells of Hangchow Bay
await your snowy craft ah Paul Verlaine
your words stowed tightly in the hold

The light that skids across the Yellow Sea
will soon falter over Peking

Solitary Man Discovered in a Field of Daisies

The sound of weeping is preferable
to absolutely nothing the man says
but nothing hears him saying so
or weeping These yellow and white

daisies get on his nerves Set the scene
with some care the usual meadow torpid
and baking in the sun that is of course
yellow and white and the daisies too

And now an odd thing occurs
where the yellow and white meet
both are lost or not lost but make
a new color that is light

The man is not cheered by this
nor does he stop his weeping O woe
O God help me he cries into the silence
that is white and yellow light

Daisies their unassailable pure form
mime of the sun the clear yellow
and rigid white the light they make
the products of endless decay

they stir to their silent rhythm
no one has ever moved or changed them
not even Wordsworth in despondency
They are yellow white to earth's last day

In Which There Is Nothing Up the Sleeve

A vague clamor attendant upon fame
well swing around a bag of apples boys
protestations are difficult and useless
what makes you think I care for summer
that water is placid Portsmouth Bay

The boys in the kitchen play hearts
summer on a blanket and two peach trees
it can be difficult without a car
boudoir poetry gets what it deserves
I am the prince of scrabbled tongues

It's too bad Clodia was a whore
Dos Hermanas Váldez cantan Mi Cafetal
avocados with a squeeze of lime juice
they make steel in Allentown Pa
a certain poet favors linden trees

Suddenly the leaves fall all at once
he is chagrined he wouldn't even know her
Christ the protestant is no friend of mine
what is the magic of music from the shore
all hearts are to be healed immediately

I once saw Mallarmé's white careful sail
the cottage rocked by brutal thunderstorms
I feel even now black lace in my hand
two people golden in the dying light
at night fragmentary words return to him

Crool Time

I ask dim questions of California friends.
That foreign sun in which the madmen grow.
O Jesus the streaked and dirty panes.
Can it be sixteen years? Where and how?
Bald heads ring the golden bay.
That green water and the mindless young.

The sleet angled with enormous cruelty.
Trembling hands touch the hotel windowsill.
The green that kills the heart in winter.
Drunk a sailor meets his drunken father.
Anything more than cheap wine by the jug?
Hey kid you look kind of familiar!

The Iceman, Again

Mixed pastries and new dresses
and sudden flights to hot San Juan.
Cousins with their coats off in the heat
drank Rheingold while the Bronx decayed.

The widow missed suppers and bought coffee
out of a machine wept long distance
into Oklahoma and Chicago.

Cold fake green of new grass and three
raw saplings snowy long before the grave
was marked. Much weeping many Protestant clichés.
Abuelita in the second car. "Thank God."

The man died apologetically maybe thinking
of some stiff suit of clothes he once appeared in
smiling for the camera almost in America.

De Pré Est Vénéneux Mais Joli en Automne

The faint blue circles underneath your eyes
have the precise tint of the lilac
and of the deadly autumn crocus.

This autumn flower violet as your eyes
flutters as your eyelids flutter
flutters in a demented wind.

The cows graze on the autumn crocus
slowly poisoning themselves
and your eyes are poisoning my life.

Children enter this vast field
to pick the faint blue flower with clamor
out of tune harmonicas faint in the wind.

The cows exit stupidly to a song
sung by the cowherd and the lilac meadow
blooms in solitude. Your violet eyes.

Verlaine's Innocents

Their high heels catching sweetly in their long sweet
    skirts
And the soft wind gusting catching at their hems
So that there were revealed a silken ankle and a calf
One ogled breathlessly. My God! we loved the game.

Sometimes a kissing bug half-crazed with jealousy
Disturbed those pale necks in the branches' shadow
In which dusk flashed sudden lightnings of white flesh
A regal banquet for ingenuous and foolish eyes.

The twilight fell ambiguous twilight of the fall
Those lovely girls dreamt leaning on our arms
Soft whispering such sweet and specious syllables
That now years later our souls still tremble in
    astonishment.

Diaghilev Did Not Say "Étonnez-Moi"

The sentimental is just outside the door
But those we love keep suffering
Sealed in a kind of immaculate truth
The odor of bouquets can't change.
The vast wilderness of nouns is seen to be
A million cruel specifics e.g.
Moon chien relámpago tyrannus.
But the sentimental never leaves
But smiles and waits with roses
Magazines assorted chocolates and news.
Enter death or defeat and humiliation
Or that sudden weariness all patience.
The sentimental evanesces but yet oh yes
Oh yes is remembered with affection
As the indefatigable visitor who came
With his goddamned ray of sunlight
With his hopeful smile in a haze of after shave.

A Celebration of Sorts

Things we place or do not place our faith in.
Newfound Jesus, politics, and corrupted art.
And all the saints and angels croon in heaven.

One's perfect hair all brilliantine
was once glimpsed on some Bermuda isle.
Oh he was the luckiest of men. He died.

Verlaine's overcoat rotted to his rotting flesh.
This was the man who invented le français?
He died too as did Beau Jack die in old Miami.

Often falling stars describe the incoherent.
On such nights it is possible to hear the sea.
On such nights the sky is navy brilliantine.

Oh listen. Listen. Listen listen listen.
That odd music is the sound of lightning.
Somewhere in the vicinity of heaven.

How tiresome to be walking on the streets
remembering the smiles of the remembered dead.
While life bashes us thank God with colors.

The Lemonade Panel

The report has come from the panel of tasters
telling us what we always knew. Everyone loves
the product made false to taste true.

Browsing. Such footnotes! Apparatus located
precisely yet with abandon. Great fields
of scarlet poppies. Good to be alive!

Situated behind this tireless grinning
is a curious world that has not lost its mind
for there was no mind: the images are war images.

The report is virginal and disaffiliated.
Objective. Cutting us down in swaths
with rootless words all antiseptic.

Meanwhile the poets are "healed
for a few dollars" and pass through each other
in gossipy vapors. Their trees are always blue.

The dark world this iron world
is but a ruptured Coney Island
ruled by that great smiling fiend.

Smiles but little laughter and data
that give little comfort or delight.
Bright headbands worn for . . . something.

By Christ they like this report they approve
they smile sang froid all mist and little jokes.
They're all right. This is the world.

Miss and Hit

We are trying to recollect specific things
To recall odd shades of purple and suddenly
There appears that crimson that recalled
Is the crimson over a city whose name we forget
Or confuse it with another city or a lake?
Staring and laboring with a specious exactitude
What appears is not the memory but a memory
Of purple that should have been there but was not
Of things and other things that were there
But at other times and so laboring and staring
We penetrate that memory and see there
That perfect world that O so perfect world
That mixes all the various ingredients
To stand unabashed as the perfect fact
Unbidden then come those immaculate purples.

"Good Night!"

She was blushing in the misty green of August
and I tell you that's a lapidary recollection
although the pitch and cadence of her voice is lost.
A lot of Christmas trees have occurred since then
and ice-skaters by the thousands dead and buried.
There shone softly a bathing suit of pastel stripes
and her thighs "kissed" so that young orthodontists
leaned and leaned smiling on her doorbell.
There is a use in shoveling through these eggshells
orange peels greasy paper bags and stinking bones
from which are stiched together songs to stun the
    drunkards.
One sees by the stars and the date on the paper
that the old year is as usual vanishing.
The dim and unintelligible smile in the department
    store
a vague and cryptic memorandum. "Get ornaments and
    tinsel."
"Have loving cup engraved." It falters in men's
    haberdashery
and the heat is too oppressive to be borne.

Où Sont Ils, Où, Vierge Souvrain?

Girls who found themselves in blue stories
given blushing words like Little Women
Did you ring sir? What are you doing?
Evening pink sun that made cold streets
just for a moment beautiful for their cheap shoes.
When they played jacks or tag and giggled
not even old bartenders could guess
that they'd appear with nothing on
but high heels and stockings and some pearls
smiling into brown Los Angeles. Such is life?
California has a real spring and who cares?
On the beach young men read *Sex-Mad Nurses*
washed down by sandy beer. You going in champ?
Indifferent lust sweeping the Loew's Alpine
threw up a thousand rose-lit boudoirs of the mind
even Mr. Walsh the drunken innocent groaned
at a private chapter of young breasts.
A waste or not a waste at all
dependent on what one considers
should have become of them. Their plain names:
Ann and Connie Mary Kate and Helen. Dolores
rapt in a black negligee her silky legs
crossed on The Boss's desk. Dolores?

The Lecture on Time and Space

An unbelievable doom tacked onto the words
Of popular songs. Hail Hail the gang!
She is all here, no? Unbelievable doom?
More poetic tricks to amaze and terrify
Your friends who all sit down at the piano
And laugh when you gesture toward a tired metaphor.
When I think of all the girls that I once knew
Strolling in summer moonlight although strolling
Is not the precise word as the laughing virtuosos know
But when I think of them when I consider them.

What was I saying? When I consider them I.
And now turning to our next subject, "The Doom of
    Words":
Thomas Nashe had a snaggletooth and was the friend
Of Robert Greene, "even in those days of license"
A spectacular reprobate. Did he know a "Diana
    Wasserman"?
That strolling girl. It's odd that Nashe describes
What could be California in Pierce Penniless
Except he left out the pianos and the supple fingers that.
You were saying something about tired metaphors.
You were mentioning "Diana Wasserman." You were
Thinking. Of Bronx roofs.

The sound of a piano
Bought on Fordham Road followed them through thin
    snow
As they made their way to the local tavern. They made
    vows
Couched in the rhetoric of popular songs. Vows to

Amaze and terrify the lowering skies. To. It was.
It was a long. It was too long ago and when I think
Of all the girls. None of them were photographed.
Doom was called bad luck in the nineteen-thirties.
And so Art does have its uses Thank you and Applause.

Everything Is a Still-Life

Out in what we may as well term thc dark
Where various memories molder their shapes snapping
From color to color from image to image
So that any articulation of any one of them is a lie
That's .where you'll find me and so you see
How easily language collapses into memory
Right before your fingertips your aging eyes

The criticism brought against me is true
I am what they say I am I admit everything
What of the tiny lakes? All the fact.
The sudden whiteness of the moon? Sure.
I take immediate dislikes to people too
Based on other people whose faces change perpetually

Not what anyone might call a good risk
Essentially nonserious vis-à-vis reality
That's to say it's all a long guffaw
How else to reconcile the armies of the fake
With tutti-frutti sunsets in the storied South?

That's where you'll find me nonchalant
A kind of perfect poster now you see me
Now you don't. The amaze is that love still lives
Forward traipsing ever forward immune to scorn
And dressed? Dressed in those old-hat clothes

Trouble in Paradise

At fifty the faces that grin in color
Or in black and white in corridors
In hallways on the gritty streets
Tax even the merest civil word of greeting.
A grievous fault. They turn and nod
Their edges smear into the background.
What background? It's your city. Choose.
The hand to the peak of the cap and a smile
Assures them of one's dogged sanity but at fifty
Why care? I don't intend to discover
What they're selling nor do I wish to see
Their souls or hearts and their minds
Exist in long passages of bad prose
In bad novels that are surely great
If not unique and of course important.
Bill is Jim or Joe and Ann is married
To Larry now or was that Sam? They have
Their troubles and it is nice to know
That they are interchangeable. They're sweet
And sad small packages of infantile desire
Looking hard inside themselves to ferret out
Some portion of the nothing in the zero
That controls the grins and that is too blank
To be tragic. At fifty I have little patience
Less understanding and my smile and word
Of pure concern blend oh how they blend
With the shabby woes that float upon our common air
As a commercial message blurred with ghosts.

The cucumber impaled upon a picket
Has no meaning whatsoever although it points
True North vaguely to the quarter ruled by love
And although it signifies precisely nothing
It has a curious reality that begs for sympathy
Which begs for idiotic poems to be written
On it and how it somehow sums up what we call
Our "plight." Or "the fix" that we are in.
There are as they say precedents for all of this
Imbecility those that come to mind right now
Are a groundhog and a plain potato though some write
Of wildflowers and of trees and Jesus knows!
It is the precise foolishness of this cucumber
Split and withered that impresses me it takes its place
Among most of the people that we know and the things
They never tire of. What I admire is that sweet jump
In sets of data that makes a flash of lightning
Occur and erases all the swill between the lines.
The bright and beautiful non sequitur the meaningless
Is where the cucumber exists a synapse
Linking mysterious but plain enormities hilarious
In their candor in their cruelty. World of steel.

The Disappearance of Oilcloth

Three young women in white dresses
At the edge of what may be a lake
And the song that issues from the vicinity
Slides across the water and has no meaning
Whatsoever. Their faces are very jolly
And one imagines them smiling as one smiles
Himself as the song is recognized. Are cheaper.
Tomatoes are cheaper. To fall in love.
Tomatoes are. Now the famous fog and mist
Borrowed from a stack of bad novels bought cheap
Covers them. Covers all. Night covers all.
Wending home. Cheap tomatoes. In love at last
With a trio of closely shaven gentlemen
In plus fours and lots of air in their heads.
It's all better than religion sweetheart
Sweetheart sweetheart will you?
We are entering the stretch of this entire
Dippy carnival. They're climbing the slope
Into the darkness of the trees. White. White.
White. A chiming laughter. No bananas today.
Tomatoes in love.

It is clear that the letters were whacked
Into the tombstones. I remember them that way
I think. Of course the weather has blurred
And softened them. And other received ideas.
Received from what? From the place where
The heart soars wild and free and we all feel
Sorry for X because B always thought that he
Was a sap if not something to wipe her feet on.
Oh world world. Is it possible ever to say
Anything that has not been spat upon by every
Liar of intelligence beneath the sun? Sun?
Sure, sun. You remember the sun that feels so
Good in winter and in summer it etcetera.
World world we are stupid in the face
Of your own precise and exquisite stupidity.
The letters on the tombstones were cut into them
With slow and patient craft. Maybe.

Cruel Experiments Continue!

If you want to mumble roses and sheet steel
Some matte and some all glitter go ahead.
Our Time on Earth is Brief and so we mumble
Anything. In his odd and glancing way
Ranford Salem speaks of the true meaning
Of things but they proliferate my God
There they are more and more of them each day.
How about the good old beaver a poor sap
Of a creature which Ranford twists and turns
And beats into a Metaphor? Matte steel roses
Into paint and paint on a glitter of wall
On which looms the shadow of a beaver hat?
A beaver hat then. What the hell. He's got
Those fucking images down pat and ceaselessly.
So Life does have a meaning after all!
Or else the thrill the pain of newfound love.
Tell it to the cockroach and God knows
Why he was put here! And so the autumn comes
Shuffling along in the same old shabby words.

Evils of the City

We have decided to accept the actual. O reilly?
Soitnly. Who recalls with faint amaze
The old turnip or some other kind of nut
About Pat and Mike meeting on a street.
In Dublin. If form is never more sez Pat
Than an extension of content then Mike adds
We'll bejayzus be contented until further orders
An Irish phrase all homely stirabout and tweed.
Was it not Lorenzo in his "Pillows of Wisdom"
Who said the penis was but a snake slipping down
An abandoned mineshaft? And if that is not the actual
Gents why bother? A position paper will in effect
Sort of be and yet is as of now or otherwise.
God. The sunny hills are slathered o'er
With tons of all this crap and yet and still
That's the trouble with the Irish and many others
Laughing all the time while life hulks by
Completely actual. And it's sex and death they laugh at
Have they no shame at all? The actual is exceeding
There and deadly glum and somber still they laugh
At that moiety of the world half muffled under crap
And though soon we will be is and make clear to be
Apparent that By Jesus through the sound of deep
Grammarians in drone Yer eye! sez Pat. And others!

Barely Aware of the Insistent Loud Roars

What then is the new surrealism and just who
Is most meaningful? What does one mean
I mean by meaningful? Who wouldn't believe
Those eyes? Are there stars? How is poetry
Used? If you know your p's and q's concerning say
Canzoni will you win the Coveted Award?

Yet is rhyme still useful? When and how?
Just what is high seriousness? If we can't be
The same old sweethearts can we just be
The same old friends? In Glocca Morra?
Is American poetry provincial and if so
Who will find the cure? Is there a cure?

Who knows? Where? Or when? And what
Do women want? What if women won't? Is there
A viable phrase in Henry Longfellow? Some
Body writes with eloquence on certain
Of the Poems does he not? Will this love of his
Fade out of sight? Can it be taken for a real romance?

Drum bingo eats bananas but does blue sky mourn?
Why do otters slipping into ponds cause huge ennui?
O gnarled and flinty lips crack corn and rice?
Or where? East Harlem? Manakoora? Are you lonesome
And sorry? What is boudoir sentiment roughed up
By Apollinaire? The night and the music?

Have you got any castles baby? En España?
Is moonlight but a coat of scum as Sappho hints?
Where'd she get those eyes? Slambango?
If the ballooning poet slogs around in robes
Of asphodel and moly thrills there a heart
That mutters to the cat Cat Cat? Can do?

What if a butch of a witch glows raffinée?
Does Chong come from Hong? Or Kong?
And has he seen Paree? If in the center
Of the jiggle bud there blows a subtle peach
Does it exist in our bouquet? If Grampa
Never read "Mauve Pears" yet grins in death?

Strambotto

I'll get along he said with blue champagne
All fizz as usual in the spooky purple light.
Those who remember white dresses are sane
And standing in the dusk with night
Charging in from Alabama and its soft plain
Of lacquered blanco glitters in the night.
Sometimes the wacky odor of the sugar cane
In old Habana blurs the speaker's sight.

But who's counting? Or separating pain
From all the laughs that flew around or might
Have flown? The past is living in the main
Right here. On umber afternoons bright
Evenings reappear in lying glamour.
His glass of azure wine her romantic stammer
Throw up the cardboard moon.
It shines in their song and the tune

Puts June in January May in Maine.
Add a toddy and a fireplace. All right?
The moon now slightly shopworn on the wane
Ekes out a few banal expressions of delight.
Write letter and pack bag. Take cab. Board plane.
Mrs. Yesterday arrives tomorrow's flight.
Why would she vacation in old Alabama?
Because she can't forget its spectral glamour?

White dresses and a birdbath and a weathervane
On some grim sunny lawn. The slick lane
Of a blacktop. We got an awful fright
When we saw the pines were cut down. Right
Darling? As if all that dimly funny drama
Meant nothing as if its rigid grammar
Floated insubstantial as if its zero moon
Belonged nowhere. Or in some rotted tune.

The Interesting Glass

It would be nice to explain some things except that
Edouard Sansdoute has already done so in his paper
"L'Eau" greeted with hisses and firebombs
In 1894. I ain't got no body is a fragment of song
As is Weep you no more sad fountains. One is
"On the Glass" and the other "On Valorizing Water."
Yet and yet. Knowing what to do and even how to
Do it guarantees nothing. For nothing is guaranteed.

All this is certainly as benignly useless
As marital quarreling it's a way to know that
Things live and "do" something or other.
I have this enormous faith in dead forms
Especially the catalogue that gets you nowhere.
What endless delight! What endless delight!
What do I care if things are "there."
My old one-dollar Baby Brownie
Knew that and did its time standing as they say
On its head. Now for some more glasses of even
Stranger shapes not even "here" yet. But soon.

The Open Boat

An old story that you can't find out about
Or understand. But the nose has its wonted place
In front of the glasses tracking the words.
They come from heaven and are anybody's
But for now just yours. Cigarettes of course.
There are swirls of enormously crude lilac
And touches of red and plenty of blue
Not a bad color of course but everywhere.
Lately the man has been strolling about
In the past and is chagrined that nothing
Will hold still. He wants to know
What the others thought and they will no more
Tell him now than they told him then.
Patch patch. Whatever is recovered
Depends on a kind of luck that must be ignored
Or it will not come anymore. Of course
Any damn fool knows that you find out
As you find out but what finally do you
Find out? Hearty praise will not negate the fact
That the perfume so carefully named was not there
At all. Was not called "L'Écume de Paris."
Patch patch. Patch. Patch patch. Erasure.

Razzmatazz

Young and willing to learn (but what?) he was the boy
With the sweaty face the boy of the *Daily News*
The boy of bananas peanut butter and lemon-lime
Who read Ching Chow waiting for the punch line
Who watched the sun more often than not a bursting
     rose
Swathe the odd haze and clumps of the far-off shore.

Who watched the sun more often than not a bursting
     rose?
"Things" were in Greek, as: the unmixed wine; thalassa!
Tears dropping into head cheese and boiled spare ribs
Lacked that notorious piquancy of the delicious tragic.
There was something to be concocted of all this trash
(But what?) if he could but avoid the stable clerkships.

The boy of bananas peanut butter and lemon-lime
Decided on certain girls beautiful in starched blouses
And imagined their confessions in the dirty dark.
And everyone grew older to A String of Pearls.
Smoke rings slid soft and creamy into creamy haze
He reached that shore and found it was only Staten
     Island.

Ching Chow, waiting for the punch line, grinned
And read a book without a title on a unicycle.
The jokes were mixed into the wild perfume of wives
And honeymoons and girls a country fair of lusts.
All this in the days when nuns were nuns and ageless
Yet somehow almost all the fathers abruptly
     disappeared.

With the sweaty face the boy of the *Daily News*
Was not real, spoke no Italian, never dined
And was in actuality Kayo or in all events his derby.
Old women with that little mick under their oxters
Crossed themselves as frozen trolleys passed Our Lady
Of Popeyes chipped plaster and a spooky babe in arms.

The odd haze and clumps of the far-off shore
My God! were buildings fallen into disrepair
And complete with rats slaving to keep their teeth short.
Quite wonderful how it all was simply there
Just there and devoid of any meaning or portent.
In the mirror he honked a saxophone and conjured
    thighs.

Young and willing to learn (but what?) he was the boy
Who found that those fabled dreams were fabled
In that their meaning was their own blurred being
Who suddenly found his alien body to be the material
From which could be made a gent or even life. Life?
Young and willing to learn oh certainly. But what?

Bright Nightgown

To wear those old moccasins with the backs
Broken down and sockless as well was a fashion
Germane to certain modes of departing. All now
Dark as the grave and silent and the streets
Though trafficked as always are not trafficked
By them. The awesome nonchalance with which things
Disappear. Not to be thought of as complaint
But as a kind of knowledge that is incommunicable
Because who cares? Who relentlessly peers
At his own materials his impedimenta Blotters
Paper flowers yearbooks photographs faces
That were young a minute or two ago and
Experience sits as it sits ten letters
Useless but to get "the story" told to prove
Again oh again and again that love although
Insanely difficult is as they say It.
A certain turn of the head the registration
Of laughter and all of it always going away
Going away as Who sits words skirling out
Of him he too seeled in a mode of departure
Stepping out smartly toward the silence death.

Printed April 1981 in Santa Barbara & Ann Arbor
for the Black Sparrow Press by Graham Mackintosh &
Edwards Brothers Inc. Design by Barbara Martin. This
edition is published in paper wrappers; there are 500
cloth trade copies; 200 hardcover copies have been
numbered & signed by the poet; & 26 deluxe copies have
been handbound in boards by Earle Gray & are lettered
& signed by the poet.

Photo: Victoria Sorrentino

Gilbert Sorrentino was born in Brooklyn, New York, in 1929, and has lived in that borough and in Manhattan all his life. He was the editor of *Neon* in the 1950s and one of the editors of *Kulchur* in the 1960s. From 1965 to 1970 he worked as an editor for Grove Press. His published work includes six volumes of poetry and five novels, as well as many critical essays and reviews. He lives with his family in Greenwich Village.